Instruction Manual for First-Time Dads

Navigate Your Partner's Needs, Decode Baby Care Basics, and Balance Work with Family Life — Even If You've Never Held a Baby Before

Joshua Lewis Sink, BSN, RN

Instruction Manual for First-Time Dads

Navigate Your Partner's Needs, Decode Baby Care Basics, and Balance Work with Family Life — Even If You've Never Held a Baby Before

Joshua Lewis Sink, BSN, RN© **Copyright 2024 - All rights reserved.**

The content of this book may not be reproduced, duplicated, or transmitted without direct written permission from the author or the publisher.

Under no circumstances will any blame or legal responsibility be held against the publisher or author for any damages, reparation, or monetary loss due to the information contained within this book, either directly or indirectly.

Legal Notice:

This book is copyright-protected. It is only for personal use. You cannot amend, distribute, sell, use, quote, or paraphrase any part or the content within this book without the consent of the author or publisher.

Disclaimer Notice:

Please note the information contained within this document is for educational and entertainment purposes only. All effort has been executed to present accurate, up-to-date, reliable, complete information. No warranties of any kind are declared or implied. Readers acknowledge that the author is not engaged in the rendering of legal, financial, medical or professional advice. The content within this book has been derived from various sources. Please consult a licensed professional before attempting any techniques outlined in this book.

By reading this document, the reader agrees that under no circumstances is the author responsible for any losses, direct or indirect, that are incurred as a result of the use of the information contained within this document, including, but not limited to, errors, omissions, or inaccuracies.

© Copyright 2024 - All rights reserved.

Family is who you choose. Thank you, Poodle for choosing me.

Table of Contents

Forward to the Reader	vii
Introduction	ix
1. THE FIRST FEW DAYS WITH YOUR BABY	1
What Happens After Birth?	2
Room-In or Nursery?	4
Ready to Go Home?	8
Preparing Your...	9
Baby Proofing Tips and Strategies	13
Key Things to Remember:	15
2. BABY CARE 101	24
Bonding With Your Newborn	24
Clean the Baby	29
Brushing Baby's Gums/Teeth	31
Dress the Baby	32
Change the Diaper	33
Swaddle the Baby	35
Massage the Baby	36
Play With the Baby	38
Deciphering Cues	39
Is It Feeding Time?	42
Is It Sleeping Time?	45
3. FOOD ROADMAP: FROM BREASTMILK TO SOLIDS	52
Breastfeeding vs. Formula	53
Tips for Handling Breastmilk	55
Tips for Handling Formula Milk	58
Infant Feeding Tips	61
Baby Feeding Guide	64
Baby Feeding Chart	64
Night Weaning	66

Weaning Tips	67
Foods and Drinks to Encourage	71
Foods and Drinks to Limit	72
4. UNDERSTANDING YOUR BABY'S MILESTONES	**78**
Milestones	80
Attachment	86
Your Baby's Check-up Schedule	90
Preparing for Doctor's Appointments	93
Vaccines: Understanding, Scheduling and Possible Side Effects:	94
5. ANTICIPATE THE CHANGES	**102**
What Will Change?	103
You Cannot Be Too Prepared	106
Tips and Preparation Ideas	109
6. STRATEGIZE WITH YOUR PARTNER	**116**
Change Can Be Challenging	117
Tips to Improve Communication	121
7. PERSONAL TIME	**128**
You Need Alone Time, Too!	129
Creating and Following a Self-Care Routine	133
It's Okay to Ask for Help	136
8. PARTNER TIME	**142**
Understanding Postpartum Depression	143
Postpartum Depression Treatment	145
Keeping the Fire Alive	147
Afterword	153
References	157
About the Author	163
Also by Joshua Lewis Sink, BSN, RN	165

Forward to the Reader

"Father is a title. Dad is a verb."
 ~ Anonymous

Dear New Father,
 Congratulations on embarking on one of life's most rewarding and transformative journeys - fatherhood. As you hold your newborn child in your arms, remember that being a father is more than just a title; it's an active role that requires love, dedication, and a willingness to grow.
 Being a dad means showing up daily, even when it's hard. It means being present, not just physically, but emotionally too. It's about the little moments - the bedtime stories, the shoulder to cry on, and the high-fives after a job well done.
 As you navigate this new chapter, remember that life's secret is giving more than you ask for or receive. Your child will look to you for guidance, support, and unconditional love. You may not always have the correct answer, and that's okay. What matters most is that you're there, doing your best and loving your child with all your heart.

Forward to the Reader

This book is designed to accompany you on your journey into fatherhood. It's filled with insights, advice, and real-life stories from dads who have been where you are now. We hope it will inspire, challenge, and remind you that you're not alone.

Once again, congratulations on becoming a father. Embrace the joys, the challenges, and the incredible privilege of shaping a young life. You will be great at this.

Best regards,
    Joshua Lewis Sink, RN
    May 9th, 2024

Introduction

Imagine cradling your newborn baby in your arms for the first time, feeling a mixture of overwhelming love and paralyzing fear coursing through your veins. As you gaze down at their tiny, fragile form, every fiber of your being is consumed by a single, terrifying thought, "Am I capable of being the father my child needs?" Despite having many extended family members close by, the reality of caring for a newborn feels like uncharted territory. The weight of responsibility bears on you, magnified by your insecurities and uncertainties. Will you be able to protect your child from harm, comfort them when they cry, and provide for them in every way they need? Countless first-time dads have stood in your shoes, grappling with the same doubts and anxieties. And while the road ahead may seem daunting, take comfort in the knowledge that with each passing day, you'll grow stronger, more confident, and more capable of rising to the challenges of fatherhood.

Over the years, the role of fathers has transformed in many ways, painting a colorful picture of modern-day parenthood. Gone are the days of the traditional breadwinner; today's dads

Introduction

come in all shapes and sizes, from stay-at-home superheroes to nurturing stepparents and beyond. Economic shifts, societal changes, and family dynamics have all played a part in this exciting evolution. With more women joining the workforce and family structures becoming more diverse, dads have seized the opportunity to embrace new roles and responsibilities. From diaper duty to bedtime stories, fathers are stepping up like never before, leaving behind outdated stereotypes and paving the way for a brighter, more inclusive future for all.

The role a father plays in his child's development is truly remarkable! Dads bring their unique flavor to parenting, offering love, guidance, and endless dad jokes. Children flourish socially, academically, and emotionally when dads are actively involved and supportive. Even if they're not living in the same home, a father's positive presence leaves a lasting impact on a child's emotional resilience. The dynamic duo of mom and dad working together sets the stage for a happy, healthy family environment. Dads, keep up the good work! You're making a positive difference in your kiddo's life! Your involvement and support shape their future and contribute to their overall well-being in invaluable ways.

As a first-time dad, it's normal to feel overwhelmed and uncertain about the path ahead. The weight of responsibility can sometimes feel like a heavy burden, leaving you questioning your capabilities and fearing that you're not measuring up. The anxiety of feeling unprepared can loom large, particularly when faced with the sheer fragility of your newborn and the daunting prospect of caring for them. Balancing work demands with family responsibilities can seem impossible, leaving you exhausted and stretched thin. And amidst all this, the struggle to connect with your baby and navigate communication challenges with your partner can feel isolating and disheartening. It's easy to feel lost in the whirlwind of father-

Introduction

hood, craving guidance and reassurance as you strive to be your best dad and partner. Rest assured, you're not alone in these struggles, and support and understanding are available as you go through this rough ride.

Before we continue, I'd like you to think about why you're reading this book. It could have been a realization that the challenges of fatherhood are more overwhelming than anticipated. It might have been a sleepless night spent fretting over your newborn's well-being or a moment of vulnerability as you struggled to soothe their cries. Perhaps it was the pang of guilt as you juggled work commitments with the desire to be present for your family or the ache of uncertainty as you questioned your abilities to navigate this new role. Whatever the catalyst, it sparked a recognition that you need guidance, support, and reassurance in your mission of fatherhood. This book is more than just a title on a shelf; it's a lifeline, a source of wisdom and comfort in moments of doubt and confusion.

Through the HELP Method of Hold, Engage, Listen, and Prioritize, this book provides a structured approach to fatherhood, offering practical strategies and emotional support. With heightened Awareness, you'll gain insights into your role, your child's needs, and your partner's experience. Integrate these insights seamlessly into your life, fostering stronger bonds and smoother transitions. Dedicate effort and time to nurture your relationships, prioritize self-care, and embrace the joys of fatherhood. This method empowers you to confidently navigate challenges, cultivate meaningful connections, and create a supportive environment for your growing family.

In this book, you'll find invaluable shortcuts to help you through this thing called fatherhood:

Introduction

1. Navigate post-birth procedures, home setups, and nursery preparations effortlessly.
2. Master bonding techniques and decode your baby's cues for confident care.
3. Understand feeding methods, equipment care, and weaning strategies for smooth feeding experiences.
4. Track your baby's development, anticipate milestones, and ace well-baby check-ups.
5. Prepare mentally and emotionally for your new role and understand the changes ahead.
6. Juggle personal and professional life effectively while prioritizing communication and teaming up with your partner.
7. Establish self-care routines and connect with fellow dads for mutual support.
8. Learn to be a pillar of support for your partner and maintain intimacy amidst parenthood's demands.

Picture yourself confidently navigating diaper changes, soothing your little one's cries, and celebrating their milestones with pride. Experience the joy of a harmonious partnership, where communication flows effortlessly and intimacy thrives amidst the chaos of parenting. This transformation wasn't easy before, but with the insights shared in this book, it has become your reality. As a seasoned dad and registered nurse, I've walked this path and understand your challenges. Trust me to guide you toward a fulfilling fatherhood journey, where you emerge as the hero of your family's story.

Chapter 1

The First Few Days With Your Baby

As I HELD my newborn baby in my arms for the first time, a surge of emotions swept over me, overwhelming yet beautifully poignant. It was a moment I had longed for, a dream that had felt distant during years of uncertainty and longing. My wife and I had traversed a journey of hope and disappointment, navigating through the complexities of infertility treatments and the emotional rollercoaster of dashed expectations. But then, in an unexpected twist of fate, we heard the glorious news —we're expecting a baby!

As I gazed into the innocent eyes of our precious bundle of joy, all the trials and tribulations of the past faded into insignificance, replaced by an overwhelming sense of gratitude and love. At that moment, cradling our newborn close to my heart, I knew our lives would never again be the same but filled with the boundless joys and challenges of parenthood.

Becoming a father is truly an amazing feeling filled with love, joy, and a sense of wonder at the miracle of life. However, it's also undeniably overwhelming, especially when looking at all the responsibilities and tasks of parenthood. There's much to prepare for and lessons to learn, from diaper changes to sleepless nights.

Fear not. This chapter is here to guide you through it all. Here, you'll discover what happens after birth—from important screenings to essential paperwork. You'll learn how to prepare your car, home, and nursery for your newborn, ensuring everything is ready for their arrival. So take a deep breath, embrace the rocky road ahead, and let this chapter be your trusted companion on the adventure of fatherhood.

What Happens After Birth?

As a dad, witnessing your newborn take that first breath is awe-inspiring. It's a culmination of anticipation, excitement, and overwhelming love as you stand by your partner, ready to welcome your little one into the world. You marvel at the miracle of life unfolding before your eyes, feeling a surge of pride and joy as your baby lets out their first cry. Even if the cry is delayed, know that it's normal and doesn't diminish the moment's magic. Your heart swells with love as you watch your partner hold your newborn close, their bond unbreakable from the very start.

As you gaze upon your newborn for the first time, you're struck by their sheer beauty and innocence. From their tiny fingers to their button nose, every feature is a testament to the miracle of creation. You feel an overwhelming sense of protectiveness and wonder as you take in every detail, knowing that this little bundle of joy is forever a part of your family.

When healthcare professionals cut the umbilical cord, you feel a profound sense of connection to both your partner and your newborn. It's a symbolic moment that marks the beginning

Instruction Manual for First-Time Dads

of your journey as a family as you and your partner embark on the adventure of parenthood together. You marvel at your partner's strength and resilience as they bring your baby into the world, feeling grateful for the opportunity to share in this sacred moment with them.

In those precious moments after birth, you have the chance to hold your newborn close, offering them warmth and comfort in your embrace. Whether through skin-to-skin contact or a gentle cuddle, you feel an indescribable bond forming between you and your baby. It's a moment of pure joy and connection as you welcome your little one into your arms, knowing that your love will guide them through every step of their journey.

Then, you witness your partner nursing your newborn for the first time, and you feel a sense of awe and wonder at the miracle of life. It's a beautiful moment of bonding between mother and child, one that fills you with pride and admiration for your partner's strength and love. You know that you'll do everything in your power to support and protect them on this incredible journey of parenthood and cherish each moment as a family.

Amidst the flurry of activity, doctors will conduct an Apgar test on your newborn. This test assesses the baby's overall health and well-being by evaluating their heart rate, breathing, muscle tone, reflexes, and skin color (Callahan Schnabolk, 2023). Each category is given a score, which is totaled to determine the baby's condition. A score between 7 and 10 means your baby is healthy, and there's not much to worry about. On the flip side, lower scores may indicate that the baby needs extra medical care. However, it's essential to remember that the Apgar test is just a snapshot of the baby's condition at birth and doesn't necessarily predict their future health.

Joshua Lewis Sink, BSN, RN

Room-In or Nursery?

Learning about what to expect is like stepping into uncharted territory, especially in those whirlwind moments after delivery. As a new dad, the surge of new information and choices can feel overbearing. But amid all the excitement, there's one decision that's all about nurturing that special bond with your little one: rooming in or providing nursery care.

Rooming in means your baby stays with you and your partner 24/7 after delivery, fostering an immediate connection that's both profound and heartwarming. It's a chance to embrace those precious early moments together, creating memories that will last a lifetime. But what about the nursery? Let's explore the tender nuances between these options so you can make a choice that's not just practical but deeply caring and heartfelt for your growing family.

The main difference between these two types of care is how much time your baby spends with you and your partner after birth. Picture this, as you and your tiny human, co-captains of the cuddle squad, embark on the most epic bonding journey of all time. That's rooming in! It's all about those heart-melting snuggles, endless giggles, and getting to know your little sidekick on a whole new level. Get ready for some serious bonding time!

Every superhero needs a break now and then, right? That's where the nursery swoops in and saves the day! It helps you get a little more shut-eye and focus on your other kids.

When deciding whether to room in with your little one or opt for nursery care, it's all about what feels right for you, your partner, and your bundle of joy. Neither choice is better or worse, they just offer different perks depending on your situation. If your baby's Apgar score was lower, the medical team might suggest nursery care, ensuring quick access to assistance if needed.

But don't worry, the medical team still has your back even if you choose to room-in! It's all about making sure you're comfortable and confident in your decision. Remember, you're not alone in this; whatever choice you make, it's all about what's best for you and your precious little one. One of the best ways to do that is to understand the benefits of both and make an informed decision. Let's break them down below.

The benefits of rooming-in include the following:

1. **Enhanced bonding:** Rooming-in fosters a deeper connection between you and your baby, allowing for uninterrupted cuddles and quality time together. These moments of closeness create a strong foundation for your relationship, filled with love and trust that will continue to grow as your baby develops.
2. **Reduced stress:** With your baby by your side, you can respond promptly to their needs, leading to a calmer and more content atmosphere for both you and your little one. This immediate accessibility eases worries or anxieties, promoting a sense of security and well-being for both parent and child.
3. **Breastfeeding support:** Rooming-in promotes successful breastfeeding by facilitating frequent and convenient feeding sessions. This can help establish a milk supply and reduce breastfeeding challenges. The close proximity allows for timely feedings, fostering a positive breastfeeding experience and ensuring optimal nutrition for your baby.

4. **Improved sleep:** Believe it or not, rooming in can lead to more restful nights. You'll spend less time worrying about your baby's well-being and more time peacefully snoozing, knowing they're safe and sound beside you. This peace of mind promotes relaxation, allowing for deeper and more rejuvenating sleep for both you and your baby.
5. **Early recognition of cues:** Being nearby allows you to better understand your baby's cues and respond promptly, strengthening your ability to meet their needs and build a harmonious routine. This heightened awareness fosters a deeper connection and understanding between you and your baby, laying the groundwork for effective communication and bonding.

The benefits of nursery care are as follows:

1. **Opportunities for rest:** Nursery care provides you with moments of respite, allowing you to recharge and recuperate after childbirth while trained professionals tend to your baby's needs. These periods of rest are essential for your physical and emotional well-being, ensuring you're able to care for your baby effectively.
2. **Assistance from experts:** In situations where medical attention or specialized care is required, nursery care ensures immediate access to trained healthcare providers who promptly address concerns. This expert assistance provides peace of mind, knowing that your baby is receiving the best possible care and support.

Instruction Manual for First-Time Dads

3. **Facilitates sibling bonding:** Sending your baby to the nursery for short intervals creates opportunities for older siblings to bond with their new family members, fostering a sense of kinship and connection. These interactions promote a supportive and loving family dynamic, strengthening relationships and fostering a sense of unity.
4. **Flexible support:** Whether you need a brief break to shower, eat, or simply gather your thoughts, nursery care offers flexibility and peace of mind, knowing your baby is well-cared for in your absence. This support allows you to take care of your own needs, promoting overall well-being and ensuring you're able to care for your baby effectively.
5. **Individualized care:** Nursery care allows for individualized attention tailored to your baby's unique needs, ensuring they receive the best care and support during their hospital stay. Trained professionals assess your baby's needs and provide personalized care, addressing any concerns or challenges that may arise. This personalized approach promotes optimal development and ensures your baby's well-being throughout their hospital stay.

Preparing for the arrival of your little one is such an exciting time, and part of that journey involves having heartfelt conversations with your partner about important decisions, like choosing rooming-in or nursery care. These discussions can deepen your bond and ensure you're both aligned in your approach to parenting from the very beginning. Remember, while it's valuable to have a plan in place, it's equally important to stay open-hearted and receptive to guidance from healthcare professionals. Their expertise can offer invaluable insights into what's best for your baby. So, as you embark on this beautiful adventure together, keep your hearts open and your minds ready to embrace whatever path unfolds before you.

Ready to Go Home?

As you prepare for this new chapter of fatherhood and take your little one home, there are a few important paperwork tasks to take care of before you leave the hospital.

First up, consider the birth certificate. This document isn't just a piece of paper; it's a legal record of your baby's birth that has held significance for years. In California, every baby must be registered with a birth certificate, and while souvenir certificates are cute keepsakes, they are certified ones that hold legal weight (*After Baby Arrives,* n.d.).

Next on the list is the *Paternity Declaration.* For unmarried fathers who want their names on the birth certificate, signing this declaration is a must. Note that this is a legal requirement in many states. It is just another step in ensuring that your little one's paperwork is in order from the beginning. Please ask the hospital staff for information pertaining to the state your baby is born.

Now, let's discuss inclusivity and support for all families, regardless of birthing style or composition. Whether you're navigating surrogacy, same-gender parenting, or adoption, there are resources available to assist you every step of the way.

Last but certainly not least, let's remember the Social Security Number. While you can choose whether to obtain one for your baby, getting one is a good idea. That way, you can claim your baby as a dependent when you file for income tax returns. The easiest time to take care of this is while filling out the birth certificate paperwork. However, if you need to apply separately, do so as soon as possible after going home to avoid potential delays.

Preparing Your...

Preparing your car, home, and baby's nursery before your little one arrives is essential for ensuring a smooth transition once you're all back home together. By getting everything ready in advance, you can focus on bonding with your baby and adjusting to your new role as a parent without the stress of last-minute preparations. Plus, having everything in place will give you peace of mind, knowing you're fully equipped to care for your newborn's needs from day one. Let's dive into preparing each of these areas to ensure a comfortable and nurturing space for your bundle of joy.

Car

Using a car seat for your little one is like strapping them into a cozy, protective cocoon for every car adventure! Studies show that they can lower the risk of injuries by a whopping 70% (Young-Hoon & Mackie, 2012). Talk about a superhero sidekick for your road trips. As a parent, you must buckle up your kiddo snugly and stay informed about potential risks.

Choosing car seats may seem overwhelming, but you'll soon get the hang of it. Just follow the tips below, and you'll be good to go (Anzelotti, 2023).

What are the Types of Car Seats?

- **Infant-only seats:** These rear-facing cocoons are designed for newborns and offer snug safety and cozy comfort, cradling your little one with tenderness.
- **Convertible seats:** Adapting as your child grows, these versatile companions evolve from rear-facing nests to forward-facing adventures, ensuring safety at every turn.
- **Forward-facing seats:** Once your child outgrows rear-facing seats, these forward-facing protectors provide security and confidence for their explorations.
- **Booster seats:** Booster seats offer a snug fit with the vehicle's seat belt, empowering your growing adventurer.

How Do I Pick a Car Seat?

- Select a seat that matches your child's needs, ensuring a perfect fit for their safety and comfort. When choosing a car seat, consider your child's age, weight, and height to ensure the seat is appropriate for their size. Look for features such as adjustable harness straps and multiple recline positions to accommodate your child as they grow. Additionally, opt for a seat with side-impact protection and energy-absorbing foam to enhance safety in the event of a crash.
- Practice installing and adjusting the seat. Follow the manufacturer's instructions carefully, and use the seat belt or LATCH system to secure the seat firmly in place. Ensure the seat is reclined at the correct angle, and the harness straps are snug but

not too tight. Regularly check the seat for proper installation and make any necessary adjustments to ensure your child's safety.
- Seek guidance from certified experts who offer wisdom and support as needed. Don't hesitate to contact certified child passenger safety technicians for guidance and support. They can provide valuable advice on selecting the right car seat for your child and teach you how to install and use it properly. Many hospitals, fire departments, and community organizations offer free car seat inspections and installation clinics where experts can help ensure your child's safety on the road.

How Long Should My Baby Be Facing the Car's Rear Side?

Embrace rear-facing seats for as long as possible, cherishing each moment of snug security and warmth they provide.

Where Should I Put the Car Seat?

- Use the back middle seat, the heart of safety and security, where your little one can bask in your love and protection.
- Avoid placing the seat in the front with airbags, ensuring your child remains shielded from unexpected bumps.

Selecting the perfect car seat with love and making each

adjustment with care will ensure a lifetime of safety, warmth, and cherished memories on the road ahead.

Of course, you'll need a few more items besides the car seat. Let's explore these thoughtful additions, ensuring every detail is carefully attended to for your little one's comfort and safety.

A stroller provides a convenient and comfortable way to transport your baby on walks, errands, or outings, while offering stability and ease of movement for both parent and child.

A carrier offers closeness and bonding opportunities as you carry your baby hands-free, keeping them snug and secure against your chest or back.

Having both a stroller and a carrier allows you to adapt to different situations and environments. Use the stroller for longer walks or outings, while the carrier offers intimacy and flexibility in crowded or uneven terrain.

A carrier enables close physical contact between parent and baby, promoting bonding and providing comfort for both. Meanwhile, the stroller offers relief for tired arms and backs during longer journeys, ensuring a more enjoyable experience for parents.

Home

Baby-proofing your home is best done sooner rather than later, ideally during pregnancy or shortly after your little one arrives. It is a way to proactively ensure your baby's safety during those curious exploration phases as they grow and thrive.

What Accidents Can Happen at Home?

Home is where children and parents make many precious memories, but it's also where children, especially the young one's, get into some accidents. Common hazards include falls, burns, drowning, choking, and poisoning. Areas such as the kitchen, bathroom, and stairs pose particular risks, along with access to toxic substances and potential choking hazards.

How Can I Prevent Accidents at Home?

Preventing accidents means being both vigilant and proactive. In other words, you should keep a close eye on your child and baby-proof your home. For example, you could install baby gates, put child locks on cabinets that contain hazardous substances like cleaning supplies, and anchor furniture to prevent tipping. Removing tripping hazards, covering electrical outlets, and creating a safe sleep environment are also crucial steps in accident prevention.

Baby Proofing Tips and Strategies

Baby-proofing your home involves a combination of practical steps and careful planning.

1. Find all the potential hazards in your home, paying close attention to areas like the kitchen, bathroom, and stairs.
2. Use safety gates to prevent your baby from wandering into specific rooms or staircases.
3. Secure cabinets containing cleaning supplies and other toxic substances, and install outlet covers to prevent electrical accidents.
4. Move heavy furniture up against the wall to prevent it from tipping.
5. Remove or secure any loose electrical cords or window blind cords that pose strangulation hazards.

6. Finally, stay up-to-date with the latest safety recommendations and periodically reassess your home for any new hazards as your baby grows and becomes more mobile.

As you're getting everything ready for your newborn's arrival, it's normal to feel anxious about possible accidents. I get it; thinking about your precious little one in any kind of distress is tough. But part of being a parent is being prepared for the unexpected, right? That's why it's a good idea to have a fully stocked first aid kit close by. It's like a little security blanket, letting you know that no matter what happens, you've got what you need to take care of your baby. Rest assured, you're doing great, and you're already nailing this whole parenting thing before it even begins! Let's take a closer look at what you might need in emergencies.

Why Assemble a Baby First Aid Kit?

Assembling a baby first aid kit is like creating a safety net of love for your little one. It's a tangible way to show your dedication to their well-being, ensuring that you're ready to handle any bumps, fevers, or scrapes that may come their way.

What Should Go in a Baby First Aid Kit?

Each item in your baby's first aid kit represents a gesture of comfort and reassurance. Start with infant acetaminophen, a gentle remedy for fevers and discomfort, and a reliable thermometer to monitor their health carefully and precisely. Remember the nasal aspirator and saline drops, which offer relief from stuffy noses and ensure peaceful breathing. Bandages and antibiotic ointment stand ready to soothe and heal any boo-boos, while gas drops relieve those tummy troubles. And with tweezers, nail clippers, and petroleum jelly, you're equipped to tend to their every need, from tiny scratches to dry skin. And don't stress; I've put a checklist at the end of this chapter so you remember everything you need to (Weishaupt, 2024).

Key Things to Remember:

As you prepare your baby's first aid kit, remember that it's more than just a collection of supplies. It's a symbol of your unwavering devotion as a parent. Keep it close at hand, ready to spring into action whenever your little one needs a comforting touch. Stay vigilant about restocking and refreshing your supplies, ensuring that your kit is always ready for whatever life may bring. Most importantly, you should share your knowledge and preparedness with caregivers, empowering them to care for your baby with the same warmth and tenderness you do (Weishaupt, 2024).

Baby's Nursery

Selecting the perfect room for your baby's nursery sets the stage for countless precious moments and sweet dreams. Consider factors beyond space, like how close it is to your bedroom for those late-night snuggles and feedings. Ensure the room is cozy, well-ventilated, and maintains a comfortable temperature year-round. It's also a good idea to think about ways to minimize distractions, such as using blackout blinds or soothing white noise machines. Creating a serene sanctuary will nurture your little one's growth and happiness.

Things to Consider as you prepare the nursery, it's important to pay attention to the room's quirks, especially in older homes. Take extra care if your home has lead paint, creaky floorboards, or thick walls that might interfere with baby monitors. Prioritize safety by addressing these concerns early on, ensuring your baby's environment is both charming and secure.

Joshua Lewis Sink, BSN, RN

When to Start Working on the Nursery?

While the excitement of decorating the nursery may be overwhelming, remember that your baby will spend more time with you in your room, especially at night. Use this time to plan and gather ideas, creating a vision for the perfect nursery. This way, when the time comes, you'll be ready to bring your dream nursery to life, filled with love and warmth.

What Nursery Furniture Does the Baby Need?

Begin with the essentials when choosing nursery furniture, focusing on safety and practicality. A sturdy crib that meets safety standards must be paired with versatile furniture to maximize the space. Let's remember a cozy corner for diaper changes and cuddle sessions. The nursery should be a haven of comfort for both you and your little one, where every piece of furniture serves a purpose and radiates love.

How to Accessorize Your Baby Nursery

Transforming the nursery into a magical wonderland is where the real fun begins. From soft lighting to adorable decor pieces, let your creativity shine. Personalize the space with keepsakes and photos, creating a space that reveals your family's unique story. Embrace eco-friendly options for a sustainable touch, ensuring your baby's nursery is beautiful and gentle on the planet.

Babyproofing the Nursery

As you prepare the nursery, safety should always be a top priority. The nursery should be a nurturing environment where your little one can explore and grow safely. So, take proactive measures to eliminate potential hazards, from electrical checks to securing furniture and decor items. By babyproofing early, you'll create a haven where your baby can thrive, surrounded by love and protection.

Baby Care Checklist

Congratulations on equipping yourself with the knowledge

Instruction Manual for First-Time Dads

of what to expect in the first few days after your baby's birth! Now, as you prepare for parenthood, it's a great idea to start creating checklists for various baby care situations. These checklists will help you stay organized and prepared for anything that may come your way, whether stocking up on diaper essentials, setting up the nursery, or planning outings with your little one. By taking this proactive step, you'll feel more confident and ready to tackle whatever parenthood throws your way.

Discharge Checklist

Before your precious newborn, it's essential to complete all necessary steps for a smooth postpartum discharge is essential before your precious newborn (Sukinik, 2017).

- Erythromycin eye ointment application.
- Vitamin K injection administration.
- Hepatitis B vaccine administration.
- Newborn bath.
- Newborn metabolic screen.
- Circumcision (if requested).
- Newborn hearing test.
- Lactation consultation for breastfeeding support.
- Infant weight and jaundice assessment.
- Gather the necessary paperwork:
- Obtain discharge notes and instructions.
- Collect any prescriptions needed.
- Fill out the birth certificate paperwork.
- Complete social security paperwork.
- Pack baby's essentials.
- Double-check personal belongings.
- Discuss any concerns with healthcare providers.

By following this comprehensive checklist, you can expedite the discharge process and ensure a smooth transition home with your newborn.

Car Checklist

Before hitting the road with your newborn for the first time, make sure you're well-prepared with these essential steps (*How to Prepare for Driving Home from the Maternity Ward*, n.d.):

- Practice installing a car seat.
- Plan baby's going home outfit.
- Familiarize yourself with car seat use.
- Adjust car seat settings.
- Limit your baby's time in the seat.
- Consider the travel system.
- Ensure an appropriate car seat.
- Pack diaper bag essentials.

Remember, safety always comes first when traveling with your precious cargo!

Home Checklist

Before the new addition to the family arrives, ensuring every room is babyproofed is essential to creating a safe environment for your little one to explore (Geddes, 2022).

Babyproofing the House

- Install detectors (carbon monoxide, smoke).
- Maintain first aid kit.
- Secure electrical outlets.
- Anchor heavy furniture.
- Check for lead paint.

Babyproofing the Bathroom

- Exterior door lock.

- Toilet seat lock.
- Cabinet locks for toxic cleaners.
- Adjust the water heater.
- Store medications safely.

Babyproofing the Kitchen

- Knob covers and door locks.
- Store sharp objects out of reach.
- Locks on lower cabinet doors and drawers.
- Unplug kitchen appliances.
- Keep wires out of reach.
- Hot dishes shouldn't be close to the counter edges.
- Clean out the kitchen junk drawer.

Babyproofing the Living Room

- Pad sharp furniture corners and fireplace hearths.
- Secure electrical and window cords.
- Install safety window guards.
- Supervise the baby closely in rooms with a lit fireplace.
- Store guns securely in locked cases out of the baby's reach.

Babyproofing the Nursery

- Keep crib free from bumpers, comforters, and pillows.
- Secure heavy furniture.
- Use an open toy box.
- Install cordless window coverings.
- Place the crib away from the windows.

Babyproofing the Laundry Room

- Use child-proof garbage cans.
- Store detergents out of reach.
- Avoid using liquid laundry gel packs until the baby is older.
- Put child locks on front-loading washers and dryers.

Babyproofing the Home Office

- Install locks on exterior doors.
- Keep small choking hazards like batteries, paper clips, and thumbtacks out of reach.

Ensuring a safe environment for your baby is essential for their safety and your peace of mind. At the same time, staying vigilant helps you identify any hazards throughout your home and address them proactively.

First-Aid Checklist

As a parent, it's crucial to have a well-prepared first aid kit to handle any small emergencies and needs (Weishaupt, 2024):

- Painkillers (acetaminophen/ibuprofen)
- Bandages (various sizes)
- Antiseptic creams/ointments
- Antiseptic spray
- Antihistamine cream
- Calamine lotion
- Gas drops
- Thermometer
- Nail cutters
- Petroleum jelly

- Scissors
- Tweezers
- Ice packs
- Saline solution

After assembling your first aid kit, remember to keep it accessible yet out of reach of children. Include a first aid manual, ensure caregivers know its location and usage, and regularly check and replenish its contents. Keep a spare kit in the family vehicle for trips!

Nursery Checklist

As you prepare your baby's nursery, consider all the necessary items to create a safe and comfortable environment. Here's a checklist of nursery essentials to help you get started (Chen, 2021):

- Crib or bassinet
- Breathable, washable mattress
- Mattress pad and cover
- Swaddles
- Sheets
- Nightlight
- Bluetooth speakers
- Lamp (or other light source) with dimmer
- Crib mobile
- Baby swing or bouncer
- Soft, easy-to-clean rug
- Playmat
- Age-appropriate toys
- Baby monitor

After setting up your baby's nursery with these essentials,

you'll be well-prepared to welcome your little one into a cozy and secure space for rest and play.

As we conclude this chapter, I'm excited to introduce you to the next stage of your parenting adventure, Baby Care 101. In this upcoming chapter, we'll dive into the invaluable realm of bonding with your newborn and mastering understanding their cues. Prepare to embark on a journey filled with heartwarming moments and invaluable insights as you nurture a strong connection with your little one.

Chapter 2

Baby Care 101

IF YOU MISSED out on prenatal classes, it's totally okay to feel a bit unsure about what lies ahead in caring for your newborn. But let me reassure you: those classes are like a crash course in baby care, offering invaluable tips and tricks you might not find online. They're a chance to learn hands-on skills and connect with other dads and experts who've been there before. While it's natural to feel a bit anxious, this chapter is your lifeline, packed with heartfelt advice and practical guidance to help you navigate the beautiful chaos of caring for your little one. From picking up your baby to decoding their cues and beyond, consider this your roadmap to becoming an awesome dad. While you might have missed those classes, don't worry, I'm here as your guide through Baby Care 101.

Bonding With Your Newborn

Bonding with your baby is such an extraordinary experience. Although it is filled with affection and love, it's okay if the connection doesn't happen instantly because it often takes time to blossom. Fathers may find their bond forming a bit later than mothers, and that's perfectly normal. No matter the pace, your baby's growth and development benefit significantly from your loving presence, whether through cuddles, playtime, or simply talking to them. No matter how small the interaction might seem, it makes a significant difference. You might face challenges when bonding. If that happens, don't hesitate to contact healthcare professionals for support. In the meantime, I've curated step-by-step advice to help you and your newborn start bonding.

Pick Up the Baby

While it might be a simple act, there are a few things to consider when picking up your baby (Morse, 2022):

1. Support your baby's head and neck while you hold them securely.
2. Avoid lifting your baby by or under their arms.
3. Keep your baby upright after feeding them; it will help with digestion.
4. Wash your hands before touching your baby.
5. Be gentle around your baby's soft spots.
6. Don't bounce your baby when they're fussy.
7. Hold your baby close when passing them to someone else.
8. Avoid sitting or lying down to hold your baby if you are tired.
9. Withhold kissing your baby if you have a fever or blisters on your lips.
10. Practice holding your baby to build confidence and comfort.

Hold Type
When to Use It

Joshua Lewis Sink, BSN, RN

Step-by-Step Instructions
Cradle Hold

- When you want to bond closely with your baby.
- During feedings or when comforting your baby.

1. Let your baby's head rest against your chest.
2. Slide one hand from your baby's bottom to support their neck. Your arm should also support the length of your body.
3. Move their head while still holding the supportive arm in place, supporting their neck, to the crook of the other arm.
4. Place your other hand under your baby's bottom (*How to Hold a Newborn: In Pictures*, n.d.).

Shoulder Hold

- When you want to support your baby's head and neck.
- During burping or comforting moments.

1. Let your baby rest against your chest and place their head on your shoulder.
2. Support their neck and head with one hand.
3. Support your baby's bottom with the other hand for added stability.
4. Avoid holding hot drinks or cooking while carrying your baby to prevent accidents.
5. Always hold your baby securely when navigating stairs or steps (How to Hold a Newborn: In Pictures, n.d.).

Belly Hold

When your baby needs to be burped or is experiencing gas discomfort.

1. Lay your baby across your forearm.
2. Their belly should make contact with your arm, and their head should be towards the crook.
3. Let your baby's feet hang on opposite sides of your hand.
4. Hold your baby at a slight angle with the head slightly upward.
5. Gently rub your little one's back to help release gas and provide relief (Marcin, 2016).

Lap Hold

When you're sitting in a chair and want to hold your baby comfortably.

1. Sit in a chair and firmly place your feet on the ground.
2. Put your baby in your lap with their head at your knees and face facing upward.
3. Lift their head by lifting your knees or holding both sides of their head with your hands. You can also put your forearms under their body for added support.
4. Ensure your baby's feet are tucked in at your waist for added stability and comfort (Marcin, 2016).

Chair Hold

When your baby is curious and wants to observe their surroundings.

1. Let your baby sit in your lap, facing the same direction as you.
2. Lean their back against your chest with proper head support.
3. Place one hand across their chest to prevent leaning.
4. Support their bottom with your other hand.
5. Provide a comfortable and secure hold (Malachi, 2024).

Football Hold

When you're feeding your baby, either standing or sitting.

1. Let your baby lay with their back against your forearm and head in your hand while supporting their head and neck.
2. With your other hand, you can adjust their head and neck.
3. Tuck your baby closer to you, allowing their body to curl against your side as if holding a football.
4. Draw them closer to your chest and offer extra support if needed (Malachi, 2024).

Face-to-Face Hold

When you want to interact closely with your baby, make eye contact and engage in bonding activities.

1. Hold your baby close to your chest, and let them face you.
2. Continue to support the head and neck with one hand while resting the back against your forearm.
3. With your other hand, support the bottom.

4. Keep your baby slightly below your chest for added comfort (Malachi, 2024).

Hip Hold

Once your baby gains control over their head and neck, it will allow them to comfortably observe their surroundings while being securely held.

1. Face your baby outward and sit them on your hip bones.
2. Wrap your arm around your baby's waist for support.
3. Your baby can comfortably observe their surroundings (Malachi, 2024).

Pass the Baby

While this isn't a hold per se, it's a good idea to know how to pass your baby to someone else.

1. Support your little one's bottom, neck, and head with both hands as you hand them over.
2. Do not release your grip until the other person has a firm hold of the baby (Shu, 2022).

Clean the Baby

Cleaning your baby is integral to caring for their health and well-being. Here's a comprehensive guide to bathing your baby, including important tips and considerations.

Preparing for bath time will make the experience both enjoyable and safe. Set up the bath area with a non-slip mat and fill the tub with warm water, ideally around 98-100°F (37-

38°C). It is a comfortable temperature for babies and helps prevent them from getting too cold.

When it's time to lower your baby into the bath, do so gently while providing adequate support for their head and neck. Using plain water for their face and a mild baby wash or soap for their body and hair ensures they stay clean and fresh. Afterward, lift them out of the water onto a clean, dry towel and gently pat them dry.

Newborns typically only need to be bathed 2-3 times weekly to keep their delicate skin clean. As your baby grows and becomes more active, bathing them more frequently, especially after messy feedings or as part of a pre-settling routine, is beneficial.

Choosing the best bath time is entirely up to you and your baby's schedule. Whether it's in the morning to start the day off fresh or in the evening as part of a calming bedtime routine, what matters most is that you're both relaxed and comfortable. A trusted adult present during bath time, especially in the early weeks, can provide an extra sense of security and support.

Essential items for bath time include a stable surface, large soft towels, a mild cleanser, clean nappies, and clothing. Depending on your preference and your baby's size and age, consider using a baby bath, a kitchen sink, or a regular bathtub.

Safety is paramount during bath time. Never leave your baby alone in the bath, even for a second. Always ensure their head and face remain clear of the water. After use, empty the bath immediately and consider taking a resuscitation course for added peace of mind.

As your baby grows, their preferences and needs may change. Older babies may enjoy splashing and playing with toys in the bath, but supervision is still crucial to prevent accidents. Watch for signs of standing or attempting to climb out of the bath, and use protective measures as needed.

When it comes to bath products, most baby bath products labeled as suitable for infants are safe to use. However, consider using soap-free options if your baby has sensitive or dry skin. Your baby's comfort and well-being are paramount, so choose gentle and nourishing products for their delicate skin.

Brushing Baby's Gums/Teeth

Ensuring your baby's oral health starts from the beginning. To prevent decay, begin cleaning their gums with a damp washcloth or infant toothbrush a few days after birth. For infants, clean their gums twice daily, especially during teething, using gentle wipes or a damp cloth.

The first tooth typically emerges around six months of age. When that happens, introduce brushing with a soft-bristled toothbrush and a grain-sized amount of toothpaste. Use gentle circular motions for two minutes twice a day.

If your baby resists brushing, try the "knee to knee" technique with a partner, ensuring one person holds the baby securely while the other brushes. Making brushing fun for toddlers can also help. Let them choose a toothbrush with their favorite color or character, play music during brushing, or tell silly stories to distract them.

As your child grows, transition to a pea-sized amount of toothpaste and supervise brushing until they're around seven or eight years old. Carefully choose a toothbrush with gentle bristles and a small enough head to fit in their mouth comfortably. Both manual and electric toothbrushes are effective, so choose what works best for your child.

Avoid U-shaped automatic toothbrushes, as their effectiveness is not well-established.

By establishing good oral hygiene habits early on and making brushing enjoyable for your child, you can set them up for a lifetime of healthy teeth and gums (*Tips for Brushing Baby & Toddler Teeth | Learn More*, 2020).

Dress the Baby

Dressing a newborn can initially feel like navigating uncharted territory for many fathers. However, with the practical tips below, this seemingly daunting task can become more manageable and enjoyable. Understanding common sizes, selecting appropriate fabrics, and mastering the gentle art of dressing and undressing will soon become second nature. From ensuring a baby's comfort during sleep to dressing for different weather conditions, these guidelines offer valuable insights into keeping your little one cozy and safe (*Dressing a Newborn—Tips and Safety Advice*, 2023):

- Newborn clothes: sizes: Common sizes include newborns, 0-3 months, and 3-6 months.
- Ensure to buy soft, cotton clothes that fit well and have low-fire danger labels.
- How many newborn clothes? Just a few items per size, as babies grow fast.
- Which clothes should I buy for a newborn? Soft, cotton, close-fitting clothes with low-fire danger labels and no loose trimmings.
- How to put clothes on a baby? Be gentle, guide arms through sleeves, and avoid pulling.
- How to dress a baby for sleep? Ensure comfort, avoid overheating, and use sleeping bags or light blankets.
- How to dress a baby in hot weather? Loose, light clothing, sun hat, and shade for sun protection.

- How to dress a baby in cold weather? Layer clothing, add one more layer than yourself, and include a hat.
- How do you keep the baby safe on the changing table? Choose a safe table, never leave the baby unattended, and keep your hands on the baby.
- Dressing and undressing newborn tips: Be gentle, distract older babies, reassure them, and use toys or songs.
- Washing newborn clothes: Use gentle detergent, separate from adult clothes, dry thoroughly, and avoid harsh chemicals. There are several brands available that are both baby-friendly and eco-friendly.

And, fellow dad, don't hesitate to reach out to experienced mothers, nurses, or parental support groups if you're uncertain about some things. They can offer invaluable advice, reassurance, and practical tips to help you feel more confident in caring for your precious bundle of joy. Parenthood is a learning experience, and with the support of those around you, you'll soon find your stride in providing the best care for your little one.

Change the Diaper

Dressing a newborn can be daunting for any new father, but with these tips, you'll become a pro in no time (Harnish, 2023).

- **Diapering essentials to have on hand:** Clean diapers, wipes, a change of clothes, diaper

wraps (waterproof coverings for cloth diapers), ointment, a loving touch, and a distraction.
- **How to tell a wet diaper from a dry diaper:** Look for indicators like a color-changing stripe on disposable diapers or a wet touch on cloth diapers.
- **How to change a baby's diaper:** Lay your baby on a clean, safe surface, unfasten the diaper, clean your baby thoroughly, dispose of the dirty diaper, and dress your baby.
- **How often do you change the diaper?** Change your baby's diapers directly after bowel movements or every two to three hours.
- **Diaper changing tips:** Keep one hand on your baby at all times, and wipe girls from front to back. Boys may surprise you with pee so be sure to keep a spare diaper or cloth handy to cover the spray. Always wash your hands afterward.
- **Baby powders and diaper creams:** Avoid talc or cornstarch powders, and use ointment sparingly unless diaper rash is present.
- **When to see the pediatrician:** If diaper rash persists after a few days or if you notice signs of infection like fever or pus, consult a pediatrician.

While these tips give you an idea of how to change your baby's diaper, you can always expand your knowledge by watching how-to videos. That way, you can see the step-by-step instructions, helping you be better prepared for the diaper-changing process.

Swaddle the Baby

Swaddling is a comforting and beneficial practice to calm babies and make them feel secure. It's such a hit that people have used it for centuries now. Below are answers to some frequently asked questions about swaddling (Andrews, 2023):

What is swaddling? It is when you snugly wrap your baby in a blanket to mimic the feeling of being in the womb. It can help soothe your baby and promote better sleep.

Why swaddle a baby? Because it mimics the coziness of the womb, it provides babies with a sense of comfort and security. It also helps to prevent the startle reflex (a feeling almost like freefalling), leading to longer and more restful sleep.

Is swaddling safe? Yes, it's both safe and effective if you do it correctly. However, it's essential to follow safe swaddling techniques and avoid overheating or restricting your baby's movement.

How to swaddle a baby: Lay a thin blanket in a diamond shape, place your baby on top with their neck along the top edge, and snugly wrap each side around their body, securing the blanket at the end.

What to do if my baby doesn't like swaddling? Some babies may resist swaddling initially, but with gentle persistence and adjustments, many can learn to enjoy the comfort it provides. Experiment with different swaddling techniques and observe your baby's preferences.

When to stop swaddling a baby: The more mobile your baby becomes, the less you'll need to swaddle. Transitioning away from swaddling to prevent the risk of suffocation or restricted movement. Watch for signs of readiness, such as attempting to roll over, and gradually introduce alternative sleep arrangements. Remember, safety is paramount as your baby grows and develops.

Massage the Baby

If you've been for a massage, you'll know how relaxing it can be. But did you know that massaging your baby can help strengthen the bond you share? There are other interesting facts, too, so let's jump right in (Curran, 2023):

Health benefits: Massaging your baby has been linked to improved sleep quality, stress reduction, healthy brain and physical development, and enhanced non-verbal communication. It can also provide relief from issues like colic, constipation, and teething discomfort while promoting relaxation and better sleep patterns.

When to start a massage: With your doctor's approval, you can begin massaging your baby from birth. It's essential to choose a time when your baby is both alert and calm, such as after changing diapers or right before putting them to bed.

How often to massage: Daily massages can be super beneficial. Pay attention to your baby's cues and adjust the duration accordingly, typically ranging from 10 to 30 minutes per session.

How to perform massage: Start by gathering your supplies, including a soft blanket or towel and baby-safe massage oil. Sit comfortably on the floor, remove your baby's clothes, and keep their diaper on. Then, follow these techniques for each body part:

- **Tummy:** Use gentle, circular motions to massage the abdomen, helping with digestion and relieving gastrointestinal discomfort.
- **Head and face:** Massage the scalp, ears, cheeks, and jaw to release tension and promote relaxation.

- **Chest:** Start stroking the chest from the T-shaped chest bone (sternum) outwardly to the shoulders.
- **Arms:** Massage the arms to improve muscle tone and coordination using gentle strokes and circular motions.
- **Back:** Massage the back with firm yet gentle strokes, promoting comfort and relaxation, especially when lying on the stomach.
- **Legs:** Lift and massage each leg from the thigh to the foot, releasing tension and promoting relaxation.

Tips for Baby Massage: Follow these general guidelines to ensure the experience is both safe and enjoyable (Curran, 2023):

- Don't massage your baby directly after feeding.
- Use gentle but firm strokes and adjust the technique based on how your baby reacts. You'll see whether they like it or not.
- Be careful not to use massage oils without consulting your doctor first. They'll tell you which fragrance-free options you can choose from.

There are how-to videos online to provide step-by-step instructions on providing your baby with this wonderful treat. Remember to relax and enjoy this special bonding time with your baby. Massage can be a rewarding experience for both of you.

Play With the Baby

Engaging with your newborn through play is not only enjoyable but also crucial for their development. To help with that development, you can play with your little one in various ways (Dumaplin, 2023):

- **Face-to-face time:** Make eye contact with your baby, stick out your tongue, or make funny faces. Babies love facial expressions, and this interaction helps build emotional bonds.
- **Talking:** Engage in conversation with your baby throughout the day, narrating your activities, such as diaper changes or feeding. This exposure to language stimulates language development.
- **Reading:** Even in the newborn phase, reading aloud to your baby can introduce them to language. You can read baby books or simply read aloud whatever you're reading at the time.
- **Singing:** Singing or playing music stimulates your baby's brain and can be soothing. Incorporate lullabies into your bedtime routine, or sing your favorite children's songs together.
- **Tummy time:** Place your baby on their tummy to promote muscle development and prevent flat spots on their head. You can do this on a firm surface or have tummy-to-tummy time with your baby lying on your chest.
- **Outside play:** Take your baby outside for fresh air and natural light. It could mean walking with them in the stroller or chilling on the lawn.
- **Simple toys:** Newborns are fascinated by high-contrast images and simple toys like rattles or

teethers. Choose toys with black-and-white patterns or high-contrast colors to capture their attention.
- **Light and music:** Incorporate toys that stimulate the senses, such as swings with music and visual stimulation. These toys can be engaging for awake times, especially during fussy periods in the evening.
- **Mirrors:** Babies love looking at themselves and other babies. Use a mirror during tummy time or hold it up for your baby to see themselves, providing visual stimulation and entertainment.
- **Independent play:** Encourage independent exploration by providing toys like play gyms where your baby can observe and explore on their own.

Of course, you are your newborn's best play asset at this phase of their life. Your interactions and loving presence are the best ways to engage and bond with your baby. Enjoy these precious moments of play and discovery together.

Deciphering Cues

Another important thing you should know in this whirlwind of parenthood is understanding your baby's cues will become your superpower. These signals, like tiny whispers from your little one, reveal their needs, feelings, and desires. Let's decipher these cues, empowering you to respond with love and confidence.

What Are Baby Cues?

Imagine your baby as a tiny communicator, expressing themselves through subtle gestures and movements. These cues fall into two categories: engagement and disengagement (*Cues*, n.d.).

When your baby is ready to interact, they'll let you know.

Engagement Cues - These cues signal that your little one is eager to connect with you, whether through cuddles, conversation, or shared activities like bathing or feeding.

- Bright eyes: Their gaze locks onto you or follows moving objects.
- Attentive posture: They may bring their hands together, grasp at objects, or exhibit smooth movements.
- Alertness: Their face lights up with curiosity, and they may engage in hand-to-mouth activity.

Disengagement Cues - On the flip side, when your baby needs a break or feels overwhelmed, they'll communicate it through these cues.

- Crying or fussing: A clear sign that something isn't quite right.
- Physical signs: These include a stiff or arched back or actively turning the body away from any stimulation.
- Changes in color: Paleness or flushing may indicate discomfort.
- Irregular breathing: Their breathing pattern may become erratic or shallow.

These cues signal that your little one is eager to connect with you, whether through cuddles,

conversation, or shared activities like bathing or feeding.

These cues are their way of saying, "I need a moment," signaling that it's time to provide comfort and reassurance.

What Might Affect Baby Cues?

Understanding your baby's cues isn't just about recognizing them; it's also about grasping what influences them. Several factors come into play (*Cues*, n.d.):

1. **Environment:** Babies thrive in calm, predictable surroundings. Loud noises, bright lights, or sudden changes can unsettle them, prompting disengagement cues.
2. **Behavioral state:** Your baby's level of alertness fluctuates throughout the day. Each state offers clues about their needs and preferences, from deep sleep to active awake.
3. **Motor function:** Pay attention to your baby's muscle tone and movement patterns. Smooth, controlled movements indicate contentment, while tense or flailing motions suggest discomfort.
4. **Psychological state:** Changes in heart rate, breathing, or skin color reveal your baby's internal state. Responding promptly to these cues helps maintain their emotional equilibrium.

By tuning into these cues and responding with sensitivity, you're not just meeting your baby's immediate needs but fostering a deep bond built on trust and understanding. Of course, these cues will tell you whether your baby needs to eat or sleep or whether it's something else. Let's take a look at how you can distinguish those signs below.

Joshua Lewis Sink, BSN, RN

Is It Feeding Time?

Feeding your little ones means giving them the nutrients they need to grow. Understanding your baby's cues will guide you like a compass, ensuring you meet their needs with love and care. Below, I've broken down feeding and cues as simply as possible.

Crying is seen as a universal sign of hunger but is often seen as a late indicator. Pay attention to cues to catch hunger early (CDC, 2019):

Hunger Cues from Birth to 5 Months Old

- Hand-to-mouth activity: Your baby may suck on fists or fingers.Hunger
- Head turning: They instinctively seek the breast or bottle.
- Facial expressions: Look for lip-smacking or licking.
- Hand gestures: Clenched fists are a telltale sign of hunger.

Cues from 6 to 23 Months Old

- Reaching or pointing: Your baby shows interest in food
- Opening mouth: They eagerly accept spoons or food offered.
- Excitement: Visual cues like hand motions or sounds signal hunger.
- Verbal cues: Some babies vocalize to express their hunger.

Cues of Comfort Nursing

Sometimes, your baby seeks comfort rather than nourishment. Watch for these signs:

- **Sucking reflex:** Even when not hungry, babies may seek comfort by sucking.
- **Cuddling:** They nestle close, seeking warmth and security.
- **Relaxed body language:** Calm, content posture indicates comfort.
- **Eye contact:** Seeking reassurance from your gaze.

Cues of Fullness

As your baby reaches satisfaction, they'll display signs of being full:

- **Mouth closure:** They refuse the breast or bottle by closing their mouth.
- **Head turning away:** Avoiding the nipple or spoon indicates they've had enough.
- **Relaxed hands:** Tension fades as they reach contentment.
- **Decreased interest:** Loss of enthusiasm for feeding indicates satiety.

Feeding Techniques

Now, let's explore the art of bottle-feeding (*Tips for Bottle-Feeding Your Baby*, 2020):

Holding Your Baby, The Feeding Process and Pacing Feeding

Keep your baby comfortably upright, supporting their head and neck - Encourage your baby to open their lips by lightly rubbing the tip of the bottle against the lips. Mimic the stop-start motion of breastfeeding by allowing breaks during feeding.

Ensure they're slightly raised, allowing them to swallow comfortably. - Prevent the milk from flowing too fast by slightly tipping the bottle. Partially remove the bottle teat to give your baby time to register fullness.

Maintain eye contact and offer reassuring words for a bonding experience. - Let your baby enjoy the feeding at their own pace, sucking and swallowing when they want. This approach prevents overfeeding and helps your baby control their intake.

Temperature Concerns

Ensure your baby's milk is just right:

- You've probably seen it on TV because it's a good tip: drip some milk on the inside of your wrist. If it's too hot for you, it will be too hot for your baby.
- Milk should be warm or cool, and never too hot to avoid scalding.
- Some babies prefer room temperature, while others may prefer warmer milk.

The Importance of Burping

Burping your baby is essential for releasing trapped gas and preventing discomfort. So, let's look at the why, when, and how of burping your little one (Bayless, 2023):

Why Burp? - Burping helps release air swallowed during feeding, reducing discomfort. It prevents gas bubbles from causing bloating and fussiness.

When to Burp - Your baby swallows air while feeding, so

burp them during feedings. Newborns may need to be burped more frequently, between breasts or every 2-3 ounces. Also burp them after a feeding to release excess gas.

How to Burp

- Choose a comfortable burping position.
- Support your baby's chest and head.
- Gently rub or pat their back.
- Listen for burps or watch for signs of relief.

When to Stop

- The more mature your baby's digestive system gets, the less burping you'll have to do.
- Around 4-6 months, you may notice a decreased need for burping.

By tuning into your baby's cues and mastering feeding techniques, you're nourishing both their body and soul. Each feeding session becomes a precious opportunity for bonding and connection.

Is It Sleeping Time?

Understanding the intricacies of newborn sleep patterns and behaviors is something every parent goes through, with both excitement and trepidation. From the get-go, their sleep becomes a central focus of their daily routine. Let's delve into the various stages of newborn sleep, from their first moments of life to their toddler years.

Newborn Sleep Needs

Newborns' sleep needs evolve rapidly during their first year. Initially, they require up to 18 hours of sleep in 24 hours, often divided into short, 2– to 3-hour sleep cycles.

Newborn Sleep Patterns and Behaviors

Newborns exhibit unique sleep patterns and behaviors that can vary from one baby to another. Frequent awakenings for feeding and short periods of sleep characterize these patterns. As they grow, babies typically develop longer periods of sleep with more defined sleep cycles.

Newborn Sleep Rhythms and Cycles

Like adults, newborns experience different sleep stages, including REM (rapid eye movement) sleep and non-REM sleep. These stages occur in cycles, with your baby spending more time in REM sleep. During this stage, your little one actively dreams, helping their brain develop and process information gathered throughout the day. Their brains are running full-speed ahead, laying the groundwork for learning and growth during their waking hours.

Settling Your Newborn

Helping your newborn settle into sleep involves recognizing signs of sleep readiness, such as rubbing eyes, yawning, or fussing. Establishing a bedtime routine can aid in this process, allowing your baby to switch off from the day's excitement and get ready for bed.

Sleep Changes From 2 to 12 Months

From 2 to 12 months, baby sleep changes significantly as infants grow and develop. Around 2-3 months, babies may start smiling and interacting more while also exhibiting longer periods of sleep. By 6-12 months, babies typically sleep for longer stretches at night, with reduced night-time awakenings.

Other Developments Affecting Sleep

During the 6-12 month period, babies may experience separation anxiety, which can lead to difficulty falling asleep and increased night-time waking. This phase is normal development as babies form strong attachments to caregivers and become more aware of their surroundings.

Night-Time Feeding

Night-time feeding remains important for babies throughout their first year, providing essential nourishment for growth and development. While some babies may gradually reduce night feeds as they approach 6-12 months, others may continue to wake for feeds depending on individual needs.

Concerns About Baby Sleep

Parents often have concerns about their baby's sleep patterns and behaviors. Remember that babies differ, and sleep variations are normal. If you have specific concerns about your baby's sleep or development, consult with healthcare professionals for supporting guidance.

Navigating the world of newborn sleep can be both rewarding and challenging. By understanding your baby's sleep needs and behaviors, you can create a nurturing environment that promotes healthy sleep habits and fosters optimal growth and development.

Is It Something Else?

Ah, the great mystery of baby cries! It's like deciphering the most intricate code! Fear not, dear parent, for we're about to embark on a journey through the whimsical world of your baby's cries, armed with love, patience, and a sprinkle of magic.

Common Reasons Babies Cry

Picture this: your baby, the tiny maestro, conducting a symphony of cries to express their needs. See some of the most common reasons for those cries below (Segal & Smith, 2024):

- Hunger
- Discomfort
- Fatigue

- Overstimulation
- Discomfort from gas
- Illness or pain
- Need for comfort

Understanding these common reasons can help you better respond to your little one's needs, providing comfort and care.

Is Your Baby Unresponsive or Indifferent?

Now, let's talk about those silent moments when your little one plays hide-and-seek with their emotions. While some babies prefer the silent treatment, ensuring they're not just taking a cozy nap in the land of zzz's is important. If you suspect your baby's gone incognito, it's time to give your pediatrician a friendly shout-out for some guidance.

Never Shake a Baby

The golden rule of parenthood is: never shake a baby! Remember, fellow dad, in the face of frustration, opt for hugs, kisses, and perhaps a spontaneous dance party to the tune of baby giggles. Shaking a baby is a hard no!

Zone in on Your Baby's Signals

In the magical realm of babyhood, communication comes in many forms. From the subtle flutter of eyelashes to the grand performance of a full-blown cry, each signal is a precious invitation to connect with your little one. Tune in to those baby broadcasts and prepare to decode the cutest messages ever!

What is Colic?

Colic is the mysterious visitor that turns your peaceful nights into a whirlwind of tears and sleepless adventures. It is a condition characterized by excessive that you can't console, even though they look healthy otherwise. It typically starts around 2-3 weeks, peaks around six weeks, and generally resolves by 3-4 months. We don't know what causes it, but we do know it's likely related to discomfort of the digestive tract, like gas or intestinal cramping (*What to Do When Babies Cry*, 2023). But fear not, brave parent, for colic shall not triumph over your fortress of love and patience!

5 S's for Soothing a Crying Baby

Dr. Harvey Karp, the wizard of baby whispering, has bestowed upon us the mystical 5 S's used for soothing even the fussiest babies (Segal & Smith, 2024):

1. **Swaddling:** Wrap your baby snugly in a cozy blanket to recreate the comforting feeling of being in the womb.
2. **Stomach or side position:** Holding your baby in these positions helps ease discomfort and promote relaxation.
3. **Shushing:** Create a soothing white noise by gently shushing near your baby's ear to drown out fussiness.
4. **Swinging:** Rock your baby in your arms or a gentle swing to lull them into a state of calm.
5. **Sucking:** Offer your baby a pacifier or let them suck on your finger to provide a comforting sensation.

With these tips, you will transform those tears into giggles faster than you can say, "Abracadabra!"

When Baby Won't Stop Crying

There might come a time when you've tried everything to stop crying, and nothing works. When that happens, thank your trusted allies, like friends, family, and fellow parents, for their sage advice and unwavering support. Together, you shall conquer the cries and emerge victorious!

Remaining Calm

It's not always easy, but remaining calm is important, especially when your baby experiences an influx of emotions. So, arm yourself with patience, sprinkle some laughter, and take a few deep breaths when everything seems too much to handle. With a heart full of love and a smile on your face, you've got this!

Know When to Seek Help

The courage to seek help is a noble quest indeed! If the cries persist and your parental instincts are tingling, it's time to call in the reinforcements. Reach out to your trusty pediatrician or a fellow parent for a helping hand and a sprinkle of wisdom.

As you wrap up this chapter, you've likely gained a deep appreciation for your vital role in bonding with your newborn. With step-by-step guidance, you now possess the tools to forge those special connections and accurately respond to your baby's cues. In chapter three, we'll navigate the exciting transition from breastfeeding or formula feeding to introducing solid foods. Get ready to embark on this new adventure of nourishing your little one's growing body and cultivating a healthy relationship with food, guided by expert insights and practical advice.

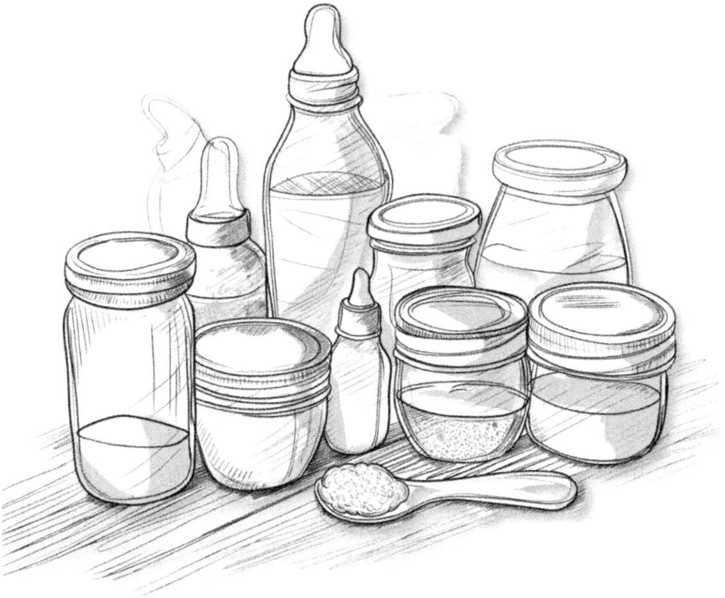

Chapter 3

Food Roadmap: From Breastmilk to Solids

PICTURE A FIRST-TIME DAD eagerly watching his partner embark on breastfeeding their precious newborn. Despite their excitement, they soon encounter unexpected bumps along the way. With determination and a touch of humor, they tackle each challenge head-on, seeking guidance from lactation consultants and trying every trick in the book to stimulate milk production. Yet, despite their best efforts, the milk supply seems to have other plans, leaving them feeling a tad bewildered but undeniably united in their quest for a solution. As they navigate the ups and downs, they find solace in each other's unwavering support and in the giggles of their little one, who seems blissfully unaware of the minor hiccups. When they finally decide to introduce formula, it's not a defeat but a joyful milestone, marking a new chapter filled with cuddles, laughter, and the sweetest baby smiles.

Meanwhile, some women may find themselves unable to breastfeed despite their best intentions. From medical conditions like insufficient glandular tissue or previous breast surgery to the complexities of medication compatibility and the challenges of substance use, there are a myriad of factors at play (Murray, 2021). Yet, amidst these hurdles, there's always room for hope and alternative solutions. Whether it's donor breast milk, specialized formulas, or simply embracing the unique journey of parenthood, the possibilities for bonding and nurturing a strong parent-child relationship are endless. So, while the path may not always be what we expect, the love, laughter, and shared moments truly define the beautiful adventure of raising a child.

Breastfeeding vs. Formula

Dads, when it comes to nourishing your little one, your partner needs all the support you can give throughout the breastfeeding process. While you won't be the one breastfeeding, your encouragement, assistance, and understanding play a crucial role in the process.

Breast milk is a superhero potion packed with all the nutrients needed for your baby to thrive. By cheering on your partner as she breastfeeds, you're helping to ensure that your little one gets the best start in life, bolstering their immune system and fostering that special bond between mom and baby.

Supporting breastfeeding means helping your partner through emotional and physical challenges. By helping with household chores, offering encouragement, and simply being there to listen, you're showing your partner how much you value and appreciate her efforts.

Now, let's talk about the challenges. Dad, breastfeeding can sometimes feel like a rollercoaster ride for your partner. From sore nipples to engorgement to worries about milk supply, your partner may face obstacles along the way.

By lending a sympathetic ear, offering a shoulder to lean on, and pitching in with diaper changes and burping sessions, you're helping to ease the journey and showing your partner that she's not alone in this adventure.

Next, we have to talk about formula feeding. While it may not offer all the magical benefits of breast milk, formula feeding can be a fantastic option for families who choose it. At the same time, formula feeding allows you, Dad, to take an active role in feeding your little one, giving your partner a much-needed break to rest and recharge. By taking over feeding duties, you're giving your partner the opportunity to focus on self-care and bonding with your baby in other ways.

Plus, formula feeding gives you the peace of mind of knowing exactly how much your baby eats, making tracking their growth and development easier. It allows you to measure every ounce you mix and every ounce your little one consumes.

Of course, there are a few challenges with regard to formula feeding, too. From the cost of purchasing formula to the extra time spent preparing bottles, it requires a bit more planning and preparation compared to breastfeeding.

But with your can-do attitude and willingness to lend a hand, you'll tackle these challenges together as a team, supporting each other every step of the way. As you do it, remember that you won't necessarily stick to the same feeding preference. Whether your partner chooses to breastfeed, formula feed, or a combination of both, your love and support remain constant. With that support, you can also enhance your partner's feeding experience by gathering the following equipment (Wisner, 2023):

- **Nursing pillow:** Supports baby and reduces strain.

- **Supportive nursing bra:** Comfortable and functional.
- **Nursing pads:** Manage leaks discreetly.
- **Nursing clothes:** Easy access for feeding.
- **Breast pump:** Share feeding duties.
- **Storage bags/containers:** Store milk safely.
- **Nipple creams/lotions:** Soothe soreness.
- **Breast shells/nipple shields:** Assist with latching.

So, as you navigate the ups and downs of parenthood together, remember that you're on this journey as a team. By offering a helping hand, a listening ear, and a lot of love, you're making a world of difference in your little one's life.

Tips for Handling Breastmilk

Before you help your partner express breast milk or handle it, wash your hands thoroughly with soap and water. To keep everything clean and safe, help clean and assemble the breast pump and its parts. Let's look at more tips for handling breastmilk below.

How to Freeze Breast Milk (*Pumping and Storing Breastmilk*, 2017)

- Store breast milk in small amounts (2 to 4 ounces) for later feedings.
- Allow one inch of unfilled space in the top of the container to accommodate expansion.
- Keep the breast milk at the back of the freezer for consistent temperature.
- Put clear labels on the milk containers with the filling and expiration dates.

- Steer clear of keeping breast milk in the freezer door to maintain consistent temperature.

How to Thaw and Warm-up Breast Milk (Pumping and Storing Breastmilk, 2017)

- Thaw the oldest breast milk first and use it within 24 hours once it has completely thawed.
- Defrost the breast milk overnight in the refrigerator or keep it under warm running water until it's back to its liquid form.
- Do NOT use a microwave to thaw breast milk, as it can create uneven temperatures and destroy nutrients.
- Warm breast milk by putting the container under running warm water or in a vessel of warm water.
- Avoid heating breast milk directly in the microwave or stove; always use water to help with the reheating process.

How to Feed Expressed Breast Milk (Proper Storage and Preparation of Breast Milk, 2022)

- Breast milk doesn't have to be warm for your baby to drink it; you can give it at room temperature, too.
- If warming breast milk, keep the container sealed and avoid direct heating on the stove or microwave.
- When breastmilk stands for a while, it can separate into a cream and milk layer. So, before you give the bottle to your baby, swirl the milk around a bit to help mix the contents.
- If your baby does not drink all the milk in the bottle, you should only use the leftovers for the next

two hours. After that time passes, discard the leftovers. It's best not to refreeze or rethaw it again.
- Always handle breast milk and feeding equipment with clean hands to prevent contamination and maintain hygiene.

How to Store Breastmilk (*Pumping and Storing Breastmilk*, 2017)

Place, Temperature, and Duration:
Countertop or table

- Room temperature
- Up to 4 hours
- Keep the containers covered and as cool as possible. Covering them with a clean, cool towel will help.

Refrigerator

- 4°C (40°F)
- Up to 4 days
- Like freezing breast milk, keeping it cool in a refrigerator works best if you put it at the back for better temperature control.

Freezer

- -18°C (0°F)
- It's best to use it within six months, but don't use it if it's been in the freezer for longer than 12 months.
- If you store the milk at 0°F (-18°C) or less, you can leave it for longer periods, but it might not be as good as breast milk stored for shorter periods.

How to Thaw Breastmilk (*Pumping and Storing Breastmilk*, 2017)
Temperature and Storage Duration:
Room temperature

- 1 to 2 hours
- Always use defrosted breast milk within 2 hours if you keep it at room temperature (up to 25°C or 77°F).

Refrigerator

- Up to 1 day (24 hours)
- If you thaw breast milk in the refrigerator at four °C or 40°F, you can use it for up to 1 day (24 hours).

Freezer

- Do not refreeze breast milk if you've defrosted it. That's because it can break down the essential nutrients or allow bacteria to grow in it.

Tips for Handling Formula Milk

If you decide to use formula milk, that's a good choice, too! There are ready-to-feed liquid formulas, along with concentrated liquid and powder formulas, that will need to be mixed. Most concentrated liquid and powder formulas follow the same instructions; however, never presume they are the same, and always follow container directions exactly. Below are a few tips to keep in mind when using formulas:

Instruction Manual for First-Time Dads

How to Prepare Baby Formula (NCT, 2019)

- **Fill the kettle:** Use fresh tap water to fill the kettle, ensuring at least 1 liter. Avoid using water you've previously boiled or that is softened artificially. That's because it has added sodium, which might be too much for your little one's kidneys to filter. I don't recommend bottled water either due to potential contaminants.
- **Boil and cool water:** Boil the water and allow it to cool for around 30 minutes until it reaches approximately 70°C.
- **Clean and sanitize:** Disinfect the preparation area and wash hands thoroughly to maintain hygiene.
- **Rinse and shake:** If using a cold-water sterilizer, rinse bottles and teats with cooled boiled water and shake off any excess solution or water.
- **Pour water into the bottle:** Add the correct amount of water to the bottle while it's still hot. Ensure the water level is accurate.
- **Add formula powder:** Follow the formula manufacturer's instructions on the packaging. When using powered formula, you will usually be instructed to fill the provided scoop loosely with the powder and level it to ensure accuracy.
- **Attach teat and shake:** Place the teat on the bottle and secure it with the retaining ring. Then cover it and shake until the formula powder completely dissolves.
- **Cool the bottle:** Let it cool down until it's the right drinking temperature for your baby. To

expedite cooling, run the bottle under cold water with the lid on.
- **Test temperature:** Before feeding, test the formula temperature to ensure it's not too hot. It should be warm but not scalding. Sprinkle a few drops on your wrist. If the formula is too hot for your wrist, it's too hot for your baby.
- **Discard unused formula:** Dispose of any unused formula after feeding. Avoid reusing prepared formula, as you can introduce harmful bacteria to your baby's system.

Storage, Tips, and Recommendations (*Infant Formula Preparation and Storage, 2023*)

- Use prepared formula within 2 hours or one hour from feeding start.
- Refrigerate unused formula immediately; use within 24 hours.
- Discard leftover formula to prevent bacterial growth.
- Store unopened containers indoors in an area that is dry and cool.
- Once you've opened it, tightly secure the lid and store it in the same dry, cool space as above.
- Use the formula container within 30 days of opening it.
- Recommendations vary based on the baby's age and water safety.
- Vulnerable babies need extra precautions against bacteria in formula.
- Different methods may be recommended, like boiling water or using sterile liquid feeds.

- Always follow the instructions from the manufacturer.
- Avoid adding extra powder or other substances to the bottle.
- Do NOT microwave formula to prevent uneven heating and burns.
- Make each feed as needed to prevent the formula from going bad.
- Consider sterile liquid feeds for premature or vulnerable babies.

Infant Feeding Tips

Properly caring for and cleaning infant feeding items is crucial to ensure your baby's health and safety. I've compiled some tips and advice to help you feed your infant correctly.

What Are Infant Feeding Items?

Infant-feeding items encompass bottles, nipples, rings, caps, and other accessories. Alternatively, feeding methods such as syringes or medicine cups may also be utilized depending on your baby's needs.

How Often Should Baby Bottles Be Cleaned?

It's essential to clean baby bottles after every feeding session. It's even better to do so immediately to prevent bacteria from growing inside the bottle.

Cleaning Infant Feeding Items (CDC, 2022)
Cleaning Method and Steps
Dishwasher

1. Disassemble components and rinse under running water.
2. Place items in a mesh bag or basket that closes when you put it in the dishwasher.

3. Switch on the dishwasher's heated water and drying cycles.
4. Place the components on an unused, clean towel and allow them to air-dry.

Hand Washing

1. Wash hands thoroughly.
2. Disassemble items and rinse under running water.
3. Wash with hot water and dishwashing detergent using a dedicated brush.
4. Rinse all the soapiness away and allow to air-dry, as with step four of the dishwasher method.

Cleaning Brushes and Basins (CDC, 2022)
Cleaning Method and Steps
Dishwasher

Follow the same dishwasher steps as with the cleaning of infant feeding equipment.

Hand Washing

1. Rinse properly and allow to air-dry after you've used them.
2. Wash every few days using the dishwasher or hand washing.
3. For infants younger than two months old, premature, or with weakened immune systems, wash after each use.

Cleaning Infant Formula Containers and Scoops

How to Clean:
Container
Wipe outside with a disinfectant wipe.
Scoop
Clean if soiled; ensure complete drying before returning to the container.

Sanitizing Infant Feeding Items (*Cleaning and Sterilizing Baby Bottles*, 2019)
Sanitizing Method Steps:
Boil

1. Disassemble feeding items.
2. Place in a pot, covering with water.
3. Boil them for 5 minutes.
4. Remove the items with tongs so you won't burn your hand.
5. Air-dry on a clean towel.

Steam

1. Disassemble feeding items.
2. Place in a steam sterilizer, ensuring space for steam circulation.
3. Add water as per the manufacturer's instructions.
4. Run the sterilizer for a specified time.
5. Store in a clean, covered container.

Drying and Storing Feeding Item Guidelines:
Drying

- Towel: Reduced risk of contamination. Allows for efficient drying.
- Drying Rack: Provides organized drying space, especially for larger quantities.

Storing

After thoroughly air-drying, assemble feeding items and store them in a clean, closed kitchen cabinet or designated area away from dust and dirt.

Baby Feeding Guide

Now we get to the age-old question: how much should you feed your baby? Well, it isn't a straightforward answer. Each precious baby is wonderfully unique, making it a tad challenging to offer precise advice. But fear not! I've gathered some guidelines to steer you in the right direction, particularly if you find yourself navigating uncharted waters, much like many of us first-time dads once did.

Baby Feeding Chart

Newborn

- 30 to 60 ml (1 to 2 ounces) - Per Feeding
- 8 to 12 - Feedings per Day

1-3 Months

- 60 to 90 ml (2 to 3 ounces) - Per Feeding
- 8 to 12 - Feedings per Day

4-6 Months

- 90 to 120 ml (3 to 4 ounces) - Per Feeding
- 8 to 10 - Feedings per Day

6-9 Months

- 120 to 150 ml (4 to 5 ounces) - Per Feeding
- 6 to 8 - Feedings per Day

9-12 Months

- 180 to 240 ml (6 to 8 ounces) - Per Feeding
- 4 to 6 - Feedings per Day

After 12 Months

- 210 to 240 ml (7 to 8 ounces) - Per Feeding
- 4 - Feedings per Day

Concerns About Overfeeding or Underfeeding Your Baby

The age-old dilemma: Am I providing too much or too little nourishment for my little one? It's natural to ponder these questions, but don't worry—you've got this! Trusting your instincts and tuning into your baby's cues is your superpower.

Overfeeding: Are you worried you might be showering your baby with a tad too much milk or formula? Take a breath; you're doing splendidly! Babies are marvelous self-regulators, signaling when they've had their fill with adorable cues, — such as turning away, slowing down, or simply drifting off into dreamland.

Underfeeding: If you're concerned about not offering enough nourishment, breathe easy. Your baby is a master communicator, subtly hinting when hunger strikes with tiny lip smacks, rooting reflex, or gentle fussing.

How to Know if Your Baby Eats Enough

Don't worry; your baby has ingenious ways of signaling contentment and satisfaction.

Watch those diapers! Aim for at least six to eight wet diapers a day in the early days, a consistent indicator of sufficient hydration.

Weighty matters: Your pediatrician will track your baby's weight gain, ensuring steady growth and thriving. Usually, a baby's weight will double by five months of age and triple by 12 months.

Happy and content: If your little one appears content, alert, and satisfied after feedings, they've likely had their fill and are ready for cuddles galore.

Trust your instincts: If concerns arise, your pediatrician is only a phone call away, ready to offer reassurance and support.

Night Weaning

Night weaning is like stepping into a new phase of parenthood, filled with anticipation and hope for more uninterrupted sleep. Typically, when your baby hits around 12 to 13 pounds between four and six months, they're primed for longer stretches without nighttime feeds (Taylor, 2022). There's no rush! Take cues from your little one and consult with your pediatrician to gauge the right timing.

Should you night wean? Gradual or cold turkey? While sudden changes might seem tempting, a gentle transition is often smoother for everyone involved. Gradually spacing out feedings or shortening each session can help your baby adjust without feeling like they've been left high and dry.

For breastfed babies, ensuring they're well-fed during the day is key. Pumping for excess helps to ease any discomfort for the breast-feeding mom. For bottle-fed babies, focus on increasing daytime feeds to reduce nighttime hunger.

Remember, consistency is your best friend here. Stick to your plan, be patient, and offer love and reassurance. If it doesn't quite work out as planned, your pediatrician can always guide and support you based on your personal concerns. With patience and determination, you and your little one will soon be sleeping through the night like pros. Sweet dreams await!

Weaning Tips

Weaning marks a significant transition in your baby's development, signifying the gradual shift from breast milk or formula to solid foods. And it's super normal to have questions about this crucial phase. Let me answer some of the common ones below:

Why wait until around six months? Breast milk, or first infant formula, gives your baby the energy and nutrition they need until around six months of age. During that time, their digestive systems get time to develop, getting ready to fully digest solid foods.

What are the signs? You will notice the following three signs that indicate your baby is ready to get their first bite of solid foods, along with their milk feedings: (*How to Start Weaning*, 2023):

1. Sitting independently and holding their head steady.
2. Picking up items with coordination of their hands, eyes, and mouth. That way, your little one can put the bottle or food into their mouth.
3. Swallowing food rather than spitting it back out.

How much will they eat? Your baby's appetite determines how much food they eat, so let your baby guide you on how much food they need, but never force them to eat (*How to Start Weaning*, 2023).

Is there a good time of day? The best time for weaning will differ for every family. As long as it suits both you and your baby, ensuring neither of you is too tired or rushed, it's a good time to do it (How to Start Weaning, 2023).

How do I wean my baby? Depending on your baby's age, you can wean them from breast milk to a cup or a bottle. Here's how you'll do it (*Weaning*, 2022):

1. Assess readiness by observing signs like interest in solid foods.
2. Choose a strategy: parent-led or baby-led weaning.
3. Start slowly by replacing one breastfeeding session with a bottle or cup feed.
4. Offer alternatives like expressed milk or formula.
5. Be comforting and supportive during this transition.
6. Gradually reduce breastfeeding sessions over time.
7. Be patient and consistent throughout the process.
8. Seek professional advice from a healthcare provider or lactation consultant if needed.

Are there different ways to wean my baby?
Weaning can take place in two different ways (*Weaning*, 2022):

1. Parent-led weaning: This approach involves the parent initiating and guiding the weaning process based on various factors such as feeding routines, medical considerations, or personal preferences.
2. Baby-led weaning: With this method, the baby takes the lead in gradually reducing breastfeeds or formula feeds, showing signs of readiness to transition to solid foods, and dictating the pace of the weaning process through their feeding behaviors and preferences.

What if my baby isn't interested in weaning? If your baby is struggling with weaning, try offering the weaning alternative before switching to breastfeeding. For example, give a bite of food before allowing them to go to the breast or bottle.

What do I need? To support the weaning process, consider having tools such as a breast pump, feeding cups, or bottles. It will allow you to introduce various liquids and solid foods to your baby.

How should I introduce my baby to solid foods?
Here are some steps you can follow (*Balancing Introducing Solids with Milk Feeds*, 2019):

As I said, in the weaning process, you can start introducing solid foods when your baby can sit upright, which is usually around six months of age.

1. Begin with single-ingredient purees of soft fruits, vegetables, or iron-fortified rice cereal. The flavor shouldn't be too complex or too quick.

2. Cook those fruits or vegetables until soft, and blend or mash them into a smooth consistency.
3. Offer a teaspoon-sized portion between milk feeds to let your baby explore.
4. Increase to 2-3 meals daily by 8-9 months, alongside milk feeds.
5. Introduce a variety of flavors and textures, including fruits, vegetables, and iron-rich foods.
6. Only introduce your little one to one new food at a time. That way, you can easily see whether they're allergic to the food or have any adverse reactions.
7. Offer small, soft finger foods for your baby to explore and enjoy.

How much solid food should my baby get, and how often should I give it? Initially, your baby will take small amounts, gradually increasing their intake as they need. Offering a variety of foods creates interest and helps develop their taste buds.

What about choking hazards? Prepare foods that dissolve easily and do not require chewing to prevent choking and avoid giving large pieces of hard foods. Here are some foods to consider:

- Soft-cooked vegetables.
- Soft fruits, like ripe bananas, avocado, cooked apples, or pears.
- Grains and serials like rice serial or iron-fortified baby cereals mixed with breast or formula milk.
- Legumes
- Smooth yogurt or cottage cheese

Instruction Manual for First-Time Dads

Foods and Drinks to Encourage

- Foods high in iron, like iron-fortified cereals
- Meat (e.g., chicken, beef)
- Poultry (e.g., turkey)
- Fish (e.g., salmon)
- Legumes (e.g., lentils, beans)
- Tofu
- Vegetables:
- Carrots
- Broccoli
- Sweet potatoes
- Spinach
- Bell peppers
- Fruits:
- Apples
- Bananas
- Berries (e.g., strawberries, blueberries)
- Oranges
- Mangoes
- Grains:
- Brown rice
- Oats
- Quinoa
- Whole grain bread
- Whole grain pasta
- Proteins:
- Eggs
- Chicken
- Lentils
- Tofu

- Greek yogurt
- Dairy (if age-appropriate):
- Cheese
- Yogurt
- Milk (for babies over 12 months)
- Cottage cheese
- Dairy alternatives (e.g., fortified soy milk)

Foods and Drinks to Limit

- Coffee
- Tea
- Fruit juice (until 12 months)
- Honey (until 12 months)
- Processed foods
- Raw or runny eggs
- Sugar-sweetened drinks
- Cow's milk (after 12 months, limited to around 500ml per day)

What about tastes and textures? Begin with smooth, mashed, or pureed foods, gradually progressing to thicker textures as your baby's oral skills develop.

Can I give finger foods for self-feeding? Introduce finger foods by 9-12 months, encouraging self-feeding. Supervise closely to prevent choking.

What if my baby is a picky eater? It's best to remain patient with your baby's changing tastes and preferences. Remember, if your baby is otherwise healthy, they just may not be ready for solid foods, or just like adults, there are some foods that your baby just doesn't like the taste. During the first 12 months of their life, continue offering various foods while breastfeeding or formula feeding. And on a sidenote, avoid foods that are choking hazards and supervise closely during meal times.

As we wrap up our exploration of breastfeeding, formula feeding, and the delicate balance of nourishing your little one, it's clear that parenthood is a beautiful tapestry woven with love, patience, and plenty of tender moments. From navigating the highs and lows of breastfeeding to embracing the convenience and flexibility of formula feeding, each family's journey is unique and special. Along the way, we've uncovered valuable insights, from understanding your baby's cues to mastering the art of handling breast milk and the formula carefully.

Now, as we turn the page to the next chapter, "Understanding Your Baby's Milestones," we delve deeper into the magical world of infant development. From those first captivating smiles to the exhilarating milestones of rolling over, sitting up, and taking those wobbly first steps, we'll guide you through each thrilling stage of your baby's growth. Get ready to celebrate every giggle, every milestone, and every precious moment as we embark on this journey together. So, grab your baby's favorite blanket, snuggle up close, and dive into the wonder and joy of understanding your baby's remarkable milestones. The adventure awaits!

Uniting a New Team of First-Time Dads!

"Of all the titles I've been privileged to have, 'Dad' has been always the best." - Ken Norton

The problem with "adulting" is that no one truly feels they're doing it right. Deep down, we all feel exactly how we felt when we were kids. We know we're grown-ups now; we see the difference when we look in the mirror, and our understanding drastically differs from what it was back then... but deep down, we *feel* the same. So when we find out we're expecting a baby, the panic sets in... Perhaps you might have had thoughts like, "I'm not ready!" or, "Aren't I supposed to be more of an efficient adult first?" Maybe you doubted whether you had it in you to be everything your child would need. Did you experience thoughts like that when you found out you would become a dad?

I promise you, you'll not be alone if you do. I don't think anyone feels ready, so resources like this are necessary. They remind you of the skills you already have and let you know what you can expect at each stage of the journey. Part of being an adult is that you never really feel like one – it's like generalized imposter syndrome! But you already have everything you need within you to be a great dad – and when you know what to expect, you can approach it with confidence.

At this point in our journey, I'd like to call on your empathy for other men with new-dad panic. Only those of us who've been there know what it's like, and it's precisely us who can make it a little easier for those who come after us—all it takes is to share information to help others feel prepared for the great adventure ahead of them.

By leaving a book review on Amazon, you'll help new readers find this information easily – and trust me, they're looking for it!

https://www.amazon.com/review/create-review/?ie=UTF8&channel=glance-detail&asin=B0D7KGKP1X

. . .

Instruction Manual for First-Time Dads

No one's prepared for such monumental change, but we can help each other through it by sharing resources and letting each other know we're not alone. All dads want this guidance; your review will help them find it quickly.

Thank you so much for your support. Go, Team Dad!

Chapter 4

Understanding Your Baby's Milestones

Milestones can be a tricky concept to grasp, especially for first-time dads. It often feels like moms have an innate understanding of these developmental markers, leaving us dads feeling a bit perplexed. Fear not fellow dad, while it's just as crucial for you to comprehend your baby's milestones, and it may seem like our female counterparts have a natural knack for this, the truth is that every parent, regardless of gender, experiences their own set of worries and uncertainties. Diving into the world of your baby's milestones is an essential part of fatherhood, one that can enrich your bond with your little one in ways you never imagined.

Picture this scenario: You're at home with your baby, and she's reaching that age where she's starting to crawl. You've read about this milestone, heard about it from friends and family, and eagerly anticipate the moment when your little one takes her first wobbly crawl across the living room floor. You're prepared. You've cleared the space, laid down some blankets for cushioning, and you're ready with your camera to capture the moment. When it finally happens, your heart swells with pride

Instruction Manual for First-Time Dads

as you witness this tiny human achieving a significant milestone. You cheer her on, celebrating her newfound mobility and independence.

Now, consider the opposite scenario: You're at a playgroup with other parents, and you notice that your baby isn't reaching the same milestones as the other babies. While babbling, sitting up, and grasping toys, your little one seems a bit behind. You start to feel the worry creeping in. Is something wrong? Or worse, am I the cause? You try not to compare, but it's hard not to wonder why your baby isn't hitting those same milestones. At this point, you may feel frustrated or even guilty, questioning your abilities as a father.

Understanding your baby's milestones means more than knowing when they should be rolling over or sitting up. It's about tuning into your child's unique growing pace and celebrating each step, whether big or small. It's about embracing the joy of watching your baby grow and develop at their own pace, knowing that every milestone reached is a testament to their resilience and your unwavering love and support as a dad.

Milestones are like the roadmap of your baby's journey through infancy and early childhood. They mark significant achievements in your child's growth and development, such as taking their first steps, saying their first words, or waving "bye-bye" for the first time (CDC, n.d.). As your baby grows, they'll reach milestones in various areas, including moving, playing, acting, speaking, and learning.

Children can develop at different paces, but most will reach specific milestones around the same age range. So, while it's important to be aware of these milestones, remember that each child's development will unfold in its own beautiful way.

As you saw from the previous examples, knowing what milestones your baby should reach and in which approximate time frame means you can keep a hawk eye on their progress.

Are they moving a bit faster or a tad slower than their peers? Armed with this knowledge, you can keep tabs on their development and spot potential greatness or areas that may need your help to improve.

For instance, if your little one reaches milestones sooner than their peers, it could be a sign that they possess exceptional abilities and would benefit from more advanced educational settings. Imagine your child's mind thirsting for knowledge and stimulation beyond what a typical kindergarten or daycare can offer. Conversely, if your baby seems slower to start talking or hitting other developmental markers, it could signal the need for intervention, such as speech therapy. Now, I'm not trying to scare you, but one of the responsibilities of parenthood is being aware of what should happen and what potential risks may arise. By being informed and vigilant, you can be better prepared for any challenges that might enter your baby's life.

Milestones

Let's take a closer look at the milestones and the timelines within which babies typically reach them. Understanding these milestones allows you to track your baby's progress and empowers you to support and nurture them through every step of their growth and development. So, below are breakdowns of the milestones you can expect in your baby's first year (Asmundsson, 2023).

Newborn Milestones

- **Week 1:** Recognizes parents' voices for comfort and familiarity.
- **Week 2:** Can focus on objects 8-14 inches away, improving eye muscle strength and tracking skills.

- **Week 3:** Starts to snuggle, adjusting posture towards comforting stimuli like parent's arms and scent.
- **Week 4:** Begins making cooing sounds and vocalizations, especially when interacting with parents, laying the groundwork for language development.

1-Month Baby Milestones

- **Week 5:** Smoother movements of the limbs and head. Encourage gentle exercises like pulling to a sitting position or tummy time.
- **Week 6:** First genuine smiles appear, with brightened eyes and upward mouth corners.
- **Week 7:** Starts understanding senses, connecting sights and sounds, and showing color preferences.
- **Week 8:** Neck muscles strengthen, allowing the baby to lift their head about 45 degrees. Encourage supervised tummy time for further development.

2-Month Baby Milestones

- **Week 9:** Fascination with sounds, especially high tones. Responds with cooing or goo-ing.
- **Week 10:** Recognizes parent's face. Your baby displays excitement with wide eyes and wiggling. Inclusion in family activities is beneficial.
- **Week 11:** Longer periods of wakefulness. May show disinterest in certain activities when overstimulated.
- **Week 12:** Your baby discovers hands and realizes that fingers and thumbs are separate. Your baby

explores by bringing hands together and putting them in the mouth.

3-Month Baby Milestones

- **Week 13:** Begins babbling, laughing, and chuckling. Displays social interactions through vocalizations.
- **Week 14:** Shows interest in toys and objects, especially those with multiple textures and bright colors. Begins grasping and batting toys.
- **Week 15:** Attempts rolling over. Safety precautions are necessary. Supervised tummy time aids in strengthening muscles.
- **Week 16:** Strengthens neck, chest, rib cage, and arm muscles. Daily supervised tummy time is required for further development.

4-Month Baby Milestones

- **Week 17:** Entertains with raspberries and laughs. Mimics sounds and enjoys interaction.
- **Week 18:** Engages in solitary play. Sharpens eyesight and depth perception. Busy with hands and eyes in play.
- **Week 19:** Begins babbling consonants and vowels. Responds to babbles by connecting sounds with meanings.
- **Week 20:** Recognizes self in the mirror and displays emerging personality traits and emotions.

5-Month Baby Milestones

- **Week 21:** Begins creeping and exploring mobility. Seeks new views and experiences.
- **Week 22:** Experimentation with objects by putting them into the mouth. Conducts tests by dropping toys to compare sounds.
- **Week 23:** Develop muscle coordination, particularly in the upper body. Progresses with assistance to standing or sitting positions.
- **Week 24:** Stores memories and recognizes names and familiar sounds. Engages in receptive language by responding to pointing and naming.

6-Month Baby Milestones

- **Week 25:** Progresses in gross motor skills such as sitting, crawling, and walking at varying rates. Requires support for sitting.
- **Week 26:** Becomes selective with smiles and may exhibit separation anxiety. Establishing routines can provide security.
- **Week 27:** Learns to cause and effect by dropping objects. Reinforces understanding of the world's workings.
- **Week 28:** Demonstrates sophisticated hand use by clapping or imitating actions. Readiness for solids includes head control, open mouth, swallowing, and doubled birth weight.

7-Month Baby Milestones

- **Week 29:** Enjoys group games like peek-a-boo. Eager for sophisticated social interactions.

- **Week 30:** Masters muscular coordination for crawling. Begins attempts at "creeping" and pushing up on hands and knees.
- **Week 31:** Develops pincer grasp for object manipulation. Fine motor skills are evolving rapidly.
- **Week 32:** Explores standing and leaning against furniture. Encourages exploration with soft landing surfaces.

8-Month Baby Milestones

- **Week 33:** Asserts opinions and preferences. Experiments with emotions and environment control.
- **Week 34:** Gains coordination and strength in legs. May pull up to a standing position. Expands vocabulary comprehension.
- **Week 35:** Strings syllables together and comprehends common words. Enhances language skills through reading and labeling objects.
- **Week 36:** Begins creating memories and setting goals. Engages in imitative behaviors for learning.

9-Month Baby Milestones

- **Week 37:** Initiate baby-proofing your home as curiosity and mobility increase. Begins exploring surroundings further and faster.
- **Week 38:** Leaves trails while scooting around the house. Engages in constant exploration and discovery.

- **Week 39:** Spends time gumming on toys or fingers, turning over, or banging small objects. Curiosity drives tactile exploration.
- **Week 40:** Observe and imitate caregiver behaviors. Mimicking is essential for learning and development.

10-Month Baby Milestones

- **Week 41:** Seeks repetition and comfort in routines. Focuses on familiar activities for self-esteem building.
- **Week 42:** Practices cruising and wobbly unassisted steps. Continues to improve leg strength and coordination.
- **Week 43:** Demonstrates understanding of object permanence. Engages in simple hide-and-seek games.
- **Week 44:** Explores stairs and furniture. Safety measures like safety gates are essential.

11-Month Baby Milestones

- **Week 45:** Prefers feeding themselves to master fine motor skills. Asserts independence during mealtimes.
- **Week 46:** Exhibits developed opinions and preferences. Expresses newfound independence in daily activities.
- **Week 47:** Learns boundaries and limitations through simple directions and demonstrations. Balances exploration with guidance.

- **Week 48:** Attempts cruising and taking assisted steps. Developing walking skills with push-pull toys and furniture support.

12-Month Baby Milestones

- **Week 49:** Experiences insecurity alongside newfound independence. Seeks reassurance from caregivers during exploration.
- **Week 50:** Establishes consistent bedtime routines for better sleep patterns. Appreciates relaxing rituals for winding down.
- **Week 51:** Learned multitasking skills by handling multiple objects simultaneously. Demonstrates growing independence and capability.
- **Week 52:** Celebrates first birthday milestone. Expands vocabulary and communication skills. Engages in language development activities for continued learning.

While keeping tabs on those milestone moments is key, remember, every kiddo dances to their own beat! Don't sweat it if your little one takes a different path or hits those markers a tad late. If you ever feel a twinge of worry, chatting with your baby's pediatrician can ease your mind. They're your go-to guide for any concerns or questions about your baby's journey. So, keep cheering on those tiny victories, and know you're doing great!

Attachment

Attachment is the profound emotional connection between a baby and their primary caregiver, often the parent who provides most of their care. It's nurtured through responsive, loving, and consistent interactions, especially during times of distress or need.

Attachment is the cornerstone of a child's emotional development, offering a secure base from which they explore the world. It helps them regulate emotions, develop trust, and build healthy relationships, laying the groundwork for lifelong emotional well-being.

For example, think about the first time you held your baby in your arms. That instant connection you felt began a bond that will help shape their sense of security and self-esteem. By nurturing this attachment, you're providing them with the emotional foundation they need to thrive in the world.

Now, you might wonder how to know if your baby is developing a secure attachment. Early signs of secure attachment include reciprocal smiles, turning to caregivers for comfort, and displaying unique responses to them. By around eight months, babies may exhibit distress when separated from caregivers, indicating a strong attachment bond.

For instance, picture you're playing peek-a-boo with your son, Liam, and every time you hide your face, he giggles with delight. His laughter and joyful expressions are clear signs that he feels safe and secure with you. These moments of shared joy and connection reassure you that Liam is developing a strong attachment to you as his dad.

Ways to Bond per Age to Develop a Secure Attachment

There are ways you can help your kiddo develop a secure attachment. But you won't try to bond with a newborn the same way you'll do with a one-year-old. So, you'll do different things depending on your baby's age. So, here are a few ways you can bond with your little one based on their age (Bartz, 2022):

- **Newborn to 3 months:** Your baby's scent triggers affection, releasing oxytocin—the bonding hormone. They recognize your face and voice and love watching your every move. Responding to cues, cuddling, breastfeeding, and massaging build strong bonds. After feedings, hold your baby close, speaking softly and making eye contact. These moments of closeness foster a sense of security, strengthening your bond.
- **3 to 6 Months:** Your baby distinguishes interactions with you from those with strangers. Consistent soothing efforts encourage exploration. Encourage hands-on play and exploration for cognitive development. Include your baby in daily activities, talking to them while you fold laundry or prepare meals. Verbal appreciation during playtime encourages their curiosity and learning.
- **6 to 9 Months:** Separation anxiety may emerge as your baby starts to remember you even when out of sight. Maintain consistent cues to build trust. Encourage communication through gestures and shared smiles. Be patient during teary goodbyes, reassuring your baby that you'll return. Respond to their gestures and share their discoveries, fostering a sense of security and connection.
- **9 to 12 Months:** Support your baby's growing sense of self by acknowledging their emotions and providing validation and comfort. Encourage social interactions with other trusted adults while reinforcing the primary caregiver bond through consistent, loving care. For example, comfort your baby when they're upset and arrange playdates

with trusted adults to strengthen bonds outside the family.

Remember, building a secure attachment takes time, patience, and unconditional love. By nurturing this special connection, you're laying the foundation for your child's lifelong emotional resilience and well-being.

What to Expect in Doctor's Appointments

Think of them as your baby's personal health tune-ups and a chance for the doctor to ensure everything's running smoothly and your little one is thriving!

These appointments are like superhero missions for your baby's health! They're where your pediatrician swoops in to track your baby's growth, development, and superhero strength against pesky germs. Plus, they're the perfect time to ask any burning questions or share your parenting triumphs and challenges.

According to the wise Dr. Chandani DeZure, a pediatric hero in Palo Alto, these check-ups are your baby's VIP pass to a healthy start in life (Miles, 2023). From ensuring they're hitting those adorable milestones to giving them the shield (aka vaccinations) they need against nasty bugs, these visits are packed with superpowers for your little one.

Well-baby check-ups aren't just about numbers and charts; they're your chance to connect with your pediatrician and build a dynamic duo for your baby's health journey. Suit up, Dads, and get ready for some superhero-level bonding with your baby's healthcare team.

By keeping up with these check-ups and sharing your superhero parenting adventures with your pediatrician, you're not only ensuring your baby's health but also building a solid support network to cheer you on every step of the way.

Your Baby's Check-up Schedule

Now that you know how important check-ups are, here's a simplified table of when your little one should go for check-ups and appointment details (Yang, 2017):

Birth

- Full examination within 24 hours to check basic functions and reflexes, measure length, weight, and head circumference, assess development and behavior, and perform a physical exam including ears, eyes, mouth, skin, heart and lungs, abdomen, hips, legs, and genitalia.
- Hearing screening (OAE and ABR).
- Newborn metabolic/hemoglobin screening.
- Immunization: Hepatitis B shot.

3-5 Days

- Measure growth, observe development and behavior, perform a physical exam, and conduct metabolic/hemoglobin screening if not done previously.

1 Month

- All basics: measurements, developmental surveillance, psychosocial/behavioral assessment, physical exam.
- Tuberculosis test.
- Immunization: Second dose of hepatitis B vaccine.

2 Months

Instruction Manual for First-Time Dads

- Same as previous appointments plus multiple vaccinations: Rotavirus vaccine, DTaP, Hib, PCV, IPV.

4 Months

- Standard procedures plus hematocrit or hemoglobin screening.
- Immunization: Second doses of RV, DTaP, Hib, PCV, and IPV.

6 Months

- Standard procedures plus additional immunizations: RV, third doses of DTaP, PCV, IPV, possibly Hib, and hepatitis B if not yet received. Consider the influenza vaccine if it is during flu season.
- Other tests may include lead screening, tuberculosis test, and oral health check.

9 Months

- Regular procedures, including developmental screening.
- Immunization: Possibly final hepatitis B dosage and third dose of IPV.
- Other tests may include oral health checks.

12 Months

- Same as usual check-up with hematocrit or hemoglobin screening.

- Immunizations: Final hepatitis B dosage, possibly third or fourth dose of Hib, fourth dose of PCV, third dose of IPV, first dose of MMR, varicella vaccine, hepatitis A vaccine.
- Other tests may include lead screening, tuberculosis test, or oral health examination.

15 Months

- Standard check-up procedures include measurements, developmental surveillance, behavioral assessment, and physical exam.
- Immunizations: Hepatitis B, Hib, PCV, IPV, MMR, varicella, hepatitis A. Fourth dose of DTaP.

18 Months

- Regular check-up procedures with autism screening.
- Immunizations: More doses for hepatitis B, DTaP, IPV, and hepatitis A if necessary.
- Other tests may include hematocrit or hemoglobin tests, lead screening, TB tests, or oral health examinations.

24 Months

- Same routine regular check-ups with developmental surveillance, psychosocial/behavioral assessment, and autism screening.
- Immunizations: High-risk children are

Instruction Manual for First-Time Dads

recommended to receive two doses of the MCV4 vaccine.
- Other tests may include hematocrit or hemoglobin screening, lead screening, TB test, oral health examination, or dyslipidemia screening.

Preparing for Doctor's Appointments

Preparing for your baby's doctor's appointments can be both exciting and nerve-wracking for parents, especially new dads. Knowing what to expect and how to prepare can alleviate some stress and make the experience smoother for you and your little one. Here are five tips for preparing for doctors' appointments:

- **Understand the vaccines:** Educate yourself about each vaccine and its purpose to feel more confident and prepared. I've created a nifty table below, along with a brief description of each disease for this exact reason. Go through it to better understand the purpose of each vaccine.
- **Comfort your baby:** Be present during the appointments so you can give your baby the comforting reassurance they need. That means stashing those worries about work and your cell phone away. For just this moment, put all your attention on your little one.
- **Communicate with the pediatrician:** Discuss any concerns or questions with the pediatrician beforehand to address any anxieties. Remember, your questions aren't silly; an educated dad is the best dad your tiny human can ask for.
- **Stay informed:** Stay updated on vaccination schedules and any changes or updates in

recommendations. In this case, it's a good idea to either have a vaccine card or create your own record. That way, you'll know exactly which vaccines your baby should get and when.

- **Be supportive:** Be a supportive partner to your partner during the vaccination process, offering emotional support and assistance as needed. It's not easy to see a needle penetrate your little one's skin, and it's equally challenging for your partner to witness. So, be there for her in whatever way she needs you. And how do you know what she needs? Well, ask her. She'll tell you whether she'd like a comforting hand or help communicating with the pediatrician.

By considering these tips, you're actively participating in your baby's healthcare, helping to ensure a positive and successful experience during doctor's appointments and vaccinations.

Vaccines: Understanding, Scheduling and Possible Side Effects:

Hepatitis B Vaccine (HepB) - Hepatitis B

- Shortly after birth
- 1-2 months
- 6-18 months
- Brief soreness and fussiness.

Rotavirus Vaccine (RV) - Rotavirus

- two months

- four months
- possibly six months
- Fussiness, temporary diarrhea, or vomiting.

DTaP Vaccine - Diphtheria, Tetanus, Pertussis (Whooping Cough)

- 2, 4, 6 months
- 15-18 months
- 4-6 years
- Tenderness, swelling, redness, fever, loss of appetite.

Hib Vaccine - Haemophilus influenza type B

- 2, 4, 6 months
- 12-15 months
- Fever, redness, and a tender injection site.

PCV13 Vaccine - Streptococcus pneumoniae

- 2, 4, 6 months
- 12-15 months
- Low-grade fever, redness, and tenderness at the injection site.

IPV Vaccine - Polio

- 2, 4, 6-18 months
- 4-6 years
- Soreness or slight redness around the site of injection.

Influenza Vaccine - Influenza

- Starting at 6 months
- Fever, aches, and a red, sore, or swollen injection site.

MMR Vaccine - Measles, Mumps, Rubella

- 12-15 months
- 4-6 years
- Rash, fever, joint aches, swelling in the neck and salivary glands.

Varicella Vaccine - Chickenpox

- 12-15 months
- 4-6 years
- Mild fever or rash, or swelling and soreness at the injection site.

Hepatitis A Vaccine - Hepatitis A

- 12-23 months
- 6-18 months apart
- Soreness at the site of injection, headache, loss of appetite, tiredness.

Meningococcal Conjugate Vaccine (MCV) - Meningococcal disease

- 9-23 months (high-risk)
- 11-18 years (booster)
- Redness, soreness at the injection site; fever (rare).

Here's a brief look at what each of those diseases are for a better understanding of why these vaccines are essential:

- **Hepatitis B** occurs when the liver becomes infected by a virus that causes acute and chronic disease. It is transmitted through infected blood or bodily fluids.
- **Rotavirus:** A highly contagious virus causing severe vomiting and diarrhea, and it mainly affects infants and young children.
- **Diphtheria** is when the nose and throat get infected by bacteria that cause a thick coating in the throat, leading to difficulty breathing and potentially serious complications.
- **Tetanus** is a condition that occurs when specific bacteria enter the body and cause the muscles to contract. It's super painful, leading to muscle stiffness and spasms, and often contracted through wounds or cuts.
- **Pertussis (Whooping Cough)** is an extremely contagious infection of the lungs, throat, and nose. It's caused by bacteria and can lead to severe coughing fits and potential complications, like fever, vomiting, and blue face, especially in infants.
- **Haemophilus Influenza type B (Hib)** is a bacterial infection that causes severe illnesses such as meningitis and pneumonia, primarily affecting young children.
- **Streptococcus pneumonia:** This bacteria causes pneumonia, meningitis, and bloodstream infections, which are particularly dangerous for young children and the elderly.

- **Polio:** Highly contagious viral infection affecting the nervous system, causing paralysis or death, primarily transmitted through contaminated food or water.
- **Influenza (Flu):** Viral infection of the respiratory system causing fever, cough, sore throat, and potential complications, especially in vulnerable populations.
- **Measles** is another contagious infection caused by bacteria that leads to symptoms like fever, cough, rash, and potential complications such as pneumonia and encephalitis.
- **Mumps,** an infection also caused by bacteria, can lead to swelling of the salivary glands, fever, headache, and potential complications such as meningitis and deafness.
- **Rubella (German measles)** is a viral infection that can cause rash, fever, and potential birth defects if contracted during pregnancy.
- **Chickenpox (Varicella):** Highly contagious viral infection causing itchy rash, fever, and potential complications such as pneumonia and encephalitis.
- **Hepatitis A:** Viral liver infection causing symptoms such as fever, fatigue, and abdominal pain, primarily spread through contaminated food or water.
- **Meningococcal disease,** caused by bacteria, causes meningitis and bloodstream infections, with symptoms including fever, headache, and potential complications.

Instruction Manual for First-Time Dads

Reflecting on the lessons learned in this chapter, it becomes clear that understanding your baby's milestones goes beyond mere observation; it's about embracing the unique pace of their development and celebrating each step forward. You've discovered the importance of being present, supportive, and patient, recognizing that every child blossoms in their own time. By tuning into your baby's cues and offering a nurturing environment, you foster their growth (reaching their milestones) and create a stronger bond between you.

As you look ahead to the next chapter, let's carry forward these invaluable insights, knowing that your role as a dad is not just to guide but to cherish every milestone, big or small, as a testament to the incredible journey you share with your little one.

In the following chapter, based on anticipated changes, you're gearing up for a new phase of parenthood. Just as you've learned to navigate the twists and turns of milestones, it's time to brace yourself for the changes that lie ahead. Parenthood is a journey of constant evolution, and as your baby grows, so must you to adapt and grow alongside them.

So, fellow dads, let's embrace the challenges and triumphs that await you in the chapters ahead. As you anticipate the changes, let's remember that each new stage brings its joys and challenges, and that's what makes this journey so incredibly rewarding. Here's to the adventures that await you, fellow dad, as you continue to cherish every moment of this incredible journey of fatherhood.

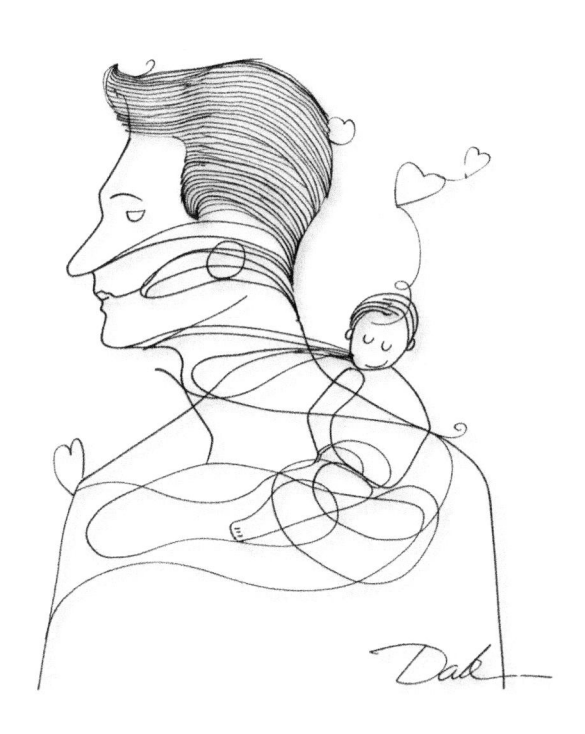

Chapter 5

Anticipate the Changes

As I REFLECT on my introduction to fatherhood, a myriad of emotions flood my heart. The joy of cradling my newborn for the first time was a surreal experience. Yet, it was tinged with a profound sense of responsibility and, admittedly, a hint of uncertainty. In that transformative moment, my hopes for the future soared, envisioning a world filled with countless firsts and shared adventures with my little one. However, amidst the excitement, doubts lingered, regrets and moments of wondering whether I possessed all that was needed for the monumental task ahead. Yet, as the days unfolded, I discovered an inner strength, a resilience that blossomed with each smile and coo from my child.

Now, as I stand on the cusp of change, I am filled with anticipation and apprehension, knowing that the journey ahead will bring both challenges and boundless blessings. With each new day, I am reminded of the immense privilege of fatherhood and its endless opportunities for growth, learning, and, above all, love. As I prepare to embrace the changes that lie ahead, I do so with a heart brimming with hope, eager to nurture and cherish every precious moment with my little one.

What Will Change?

Becoming a father is an extraordinary transformation, one that extends far beyond the visible changes in a baby's nursery. As you welcome your little one into the world, prepare for a journey of profound physical, mental, and emotional evolution. Science reveals that the very essence of fatherhood triggers remarkable shifts within you, shaping your body and brain to embrace parenthood's joys and challenges.

Let's delve deeper into the psychological aspects of the physical, mental, and emotional changes fathers may experience:

Physical changes include the following (Joormann, 2023):

- **Decrease in testosterone levels:** Research indicates that new fathers often experience a decrease in testosterone levels, particularly during their partner's pregnancy and immediately after childbirth. This hormonal shift is associated with increased empathy, sensitivity, and a desire to be more involved in caregiving. Lower testosterone levels contribute to higher levels of oxytocin, promoting bonding and nurturing behaviors towards the baby.
- **Increase in oxytocin levels:** Following the birth of their baby, fathers typically experience elevated levels of oxytocin, also known as the "love hormone." It is important to promote promoting physical and emotional closeness between fathers and their infants, fostering bonding and

attachment. Fathers who engage in caregiving activities, such as playing and skin-to-skin contact, tend to have higher oxytocin levels, further strengthening the father-infant bond.
- **Changes in cortisol levels:** When fathers hear an infant crying, their bodies produce more cortisol, a hormone associated with stress. This temporary increase in cortisol helps fathers rapidly detect and respond to infant distress, highlighting the biological mechanisms underlying caregiving behavior. Conversely, fathers experience decreased cortisol levels when engaging in comforting interactions with their infants, reinforcing attentive caregiving behaviors and emotional connection.

You might have experienced the following mental changes (LoMonaco, 2022):

- **Increased sense of responsibility:** Fatherhood increases the sense of responsibility for providing and caring for the family. As fathers transition into their role as caregivers, they often experience a shift in priorities and a heightened awareness of the well-being of their partner and child. This sense of responsibility motivates fathers to actively engage in caregiving and participate in nurturing their children.
- **Heightened emotional sensitivity:** Hormonal changes, such as increased oxytocin levels, contribute to heightened emotional sensitivity in fathers, enabling them to respond more empathetically to their baby's needs. Fathers become more attuned to their infant's cues and

signals, fostering a deeper understanding of their child's emotions and fostering a supportive and nurturing environment.

- **Improved communication skills:** Fatherhood provides opportunities for fathers to develop and refine their communication skills, both verbal and nonverbal. Knowing how to communicate effectively is crucial to fostering a strong relationship with your child and helping your child promote healthy emotional development. Fathers learn to express their emotions openly and listen attentively to their children, fostering positive communication patterns and strengthening the father-infant bond.

Finally, the following emotional changes occur (LoMonaco, 2022):

- **Deepened bond with the baby:** Hormonal changes, such as increased oxytocin levels, facilitate the formation of a deep emotional bond between fathers and their infants. Fathers experience a profound sense of love, connection, and attachment to their children, nurturing a lifelong bond based on mutual trust and affection.
- **Heightened sense of fulfillment:** Fatherhood brings about a heightened sense of fulfillment and purpose as fathers embrace their role as caregivers and nurturers. The joy and satisfaction from witnessing their child's growth and development contribute to a profound sense of pride and fulfillment, enriching the father's emotional well-being.

- **Increased empathy and compassion:** Hormonal changes, along with the experience of caregiving, foster increased empathy and compassion in fathers. Fathers become more sensitive to their child's emotions and needs, offering comfort, support, and understanding. Heightened empathy strengthens the father-infant bond and promotes healthy emotional development in the child.

The physical, mental, and emotional changes experienced by fathers reflect the transformative nature of parenthood, shaping them into more patient, empathetic, and loving caregivers. Through active engagement in caregiving activities and a commitment to nurturing their child's development, fathers embark on a journey of personal growth and self-discovery, enriching their lives and the lives of their loved ones in profound ways.

You Cannot Be Too Prepared

If it isn't clear by now, parenthood is a wild ride. Unfortunately, you'll never be as prepared as you think you are. No one is, whether it's their firstborn or the third. With every little life that comes into this world, so does a cascade of obstacles and challenges. However, let's stick to the role of being a first-time dad: Adjusting to being a father can be super challenging. While you might have your checklists and equipment ready, you might not know what to expect on a mental and emotional level.

You've nailed diaper changes, and your baby's laughter fills the room. Yet, sometimes, the weight of fatherhood feels like a mountain. That's likely because you want to take this emotional toll and handle it yourself. Luckily, you don't need to do this alone. Perinatal mental health can be like sailing uncharted waters, but with the right support, you'll emerge even stronger and more resilient than before.

Now, you might wonder what triggers those "dad-down" moments. From sleepless nights to the unpredictable twists and turns of family life, parenthood is a rollercoaster ride. Add society's relentless expectations of the perfect dad, and it can feel like carrying the weight of the world on your shoulders. Ten percent of dads experience anxiety or stress (*Adjusting to Change: Expecting and New Dads*, n.d.).

I want to hazard a guess that you're feeling tired, irritable, and maybe even a little overwhelmed, struggling with headaches, body pains, and perhaps changes in your appetite. Welcome to the club, Dad! Parenthood has a way of pushing us to our limits and can cause pretty rough feelings of anxiety, anger, and a loss of libido. Whether it's reaching out to your trusted healthcare providers, confiding in your partner, or connecting with fellow dads who've been in your shoes, there's a whole army of support waiting to lift you and help you through those tough times.

Unfortunately, most dads don't catch paternal depression early enough. It could be that they just don't know about it, like the causes or risk factors. That's because they don't see healthcare professionals as often as the mom does. To make it worse, dads can start experiencing these feelings during pregnancy, and they tend to get worse after the baby is born.

First, causes include a lack of social and emotional support and the stress of adjusting to parenthood, which can leave you feeling adrift in choppy waters. Add in relationship strains, worries about meeting expectations, and the weight of financial stresses, and it's no wonder you might feel overwhelmed.

Next, let's look at the risk factors for paternal depression. There are so many, and it could feel daunting to notice them all. From a partner experiencing postnatal depression to grappling with your history of depression, the road to fatherhood is filled with obstacles. Throw in relationship woes, low self-esteem, and the challenges of first-time fatherhood, and it's easy to see how the odds might feel stacked against you. But here's the thing: you're not alone. With the right support and a willingness to seek help when needed, you can weather any storm and emerge stronger on the other side.

With that knowledge, you can pinpoint this pesky mental struggle early enough and get the help you need. But it's essential to remember that there's no one-size-fits-all approach to mental health recovery. What works for one dad may not work for you, and that's perfectly okay! Whether seeking professional counseling, practicing self-care techniques, or simply carving out some time to recharge, it's crucial to find what works best for you and your unique journey through fatherhood. Some other methods you can try are talking to your doctor for advice or getting involved in paternal support groups.

Whichever method you choose, lean on your fellow dads, share your experiences, and uplift each other. Parenthood is a wild ride, but with a solid support system and a positive attitude, you can tackle anything that comes your way. From late-night feedings to diaper blowouts, you've got this because you're stronger than you could ever be alone.

Tips and Preparation Ideas

Sure, having everything set up for the baby is important, but there's more to preparation than just assembling cribs and changing tables. Being prepared in terms of your health and fitness, staying on top of domestic tasks, nurturing your relationships, managing your finances, and honing your parenting skills can all help you feel more confident and capable as you embark on this journey into fatherhood. We'll have a deeper look into each of these areas, but just know that there are plenty of ways you can proactively prepare yourself for the challenges and joys.

Health and Fitness

Preparing for the physical demands of fatherhood goes beyond just getting ready for diaper changes and late-night feedings. You'll find yourself lifting car seats, chasing after little ones as they explore the world, and giving piggyback rides around the house. These everyday tasks may seem small, but they require strength, agility, and endurance. Get ready to be your child's jungle gym and superhero all rolled into one with the following tips (*Preparing for Fatherhood*, 2022):

- **Prioritize nutrition:** When you start building healthy eating habits, you'll have the stamina and energy needed for fatherhood. A balanced diet can also help manage stress levels and improve overall welfare. So, consider incorporating more vegetables, fruits, whole grains, and lean proteins into your meals.
- **Stay active:** Regular exercise is crucial for maintaining physical and mental health. Even if your schedule is tight, find ways to incorporate physical activity into your routine, whether it's

taking a daily walk, doing bodyweight exercises at home, or joining a virtual fitness class.
- **Prioritize sleep:** Quality sleep is essential for overall well-being and will become even more crucial once your baby arrives. It might be challenging with a crying baby but try to establish a nighttime routine. You can do that by creating a cozy sleep environment to improve the quality of your sleep.
- **Manage stress:** Parenthood comes with its share of stressors, so it's essential to develop healthy coping mechanisms now. Try meditation or other stress-relief techniques to help you stay calm and present.
- **Monitor mental health:** Monitor your emotional well-being and seek support if needed. Openly talk to your partner about your feelings, and consider contacting a therapist for additional support.

With these tips, you can ensure you're physically prepared for the demands of fatherhood, which is crucial for navigating the journey ahead with confidence and vitality. By focusing on nutrition, exercise, sleep, stress management, and mental health, you can better handle any challenge that fatherhood throws you. Making this self-care a priority isn't selfish. You are investing in becoming the best father and partner you can be.

Domestic Tasks

Preparing your home for your baby to arrive doesn't mean you'll just assemble baby gear. There are a few other domestic tasks you should think about. They include the following (*Preparing for Fatherhood*, 2022):

- Meal prep: Stock your freezer with homemade meals that can be easily reheated and enjoyed during those hectic first weeks with a newborn.
- Babyproof your home: Take steps to babyproof your living space to minimize potential hazards and create a safe environment for your little one to explore.
- Choose essential baby gear: Focus on purchasing essential baby gear that will meet your baby's needs without overwhelming your space or budget.
- Declutter and organize: Get rid of unnecessary clutter and start organizing your living space to make room for baby essentials.
- Deep clean: Give your home a thorough cleaning to create a healthy and hygienic environment for your newborn.

Relationships

Maintaining strong relationships with your partner, friends, and family is essential as you navigate the joys and challenges of fatherhood. Here are a few ways you can cultivate these relationships and build a support network (*Preparing for Fatherhood*, 2022):

- Communicate openly: When talking to your partner, be honest and open about your expectations, concerns, and needs as you prepare for parenthood together.
- Prioritize quality time: Make meaningful connections with your partner and loved ones, even amidst the busyness of preparing for your baby's arrival.

- Seek Support: Don't be afraid to look to your support network for help and guidance as you navigate the transition to fatherhood.
- Manage expectations: Be realistic about the changes and challenges that parenthood may bring to your relationships, and work with your partner to navigate these changes as a team.
- Celebrate milestones: Take time to celebrate important milestones and achievements with your partner and loved ones, whether it's a positive pregnancy test, a successful ultrasound, or a completed nursery project.

In this chapter, we explored the profound changes accompanying the transition to fatherhood, encompassing physical, mental, and emotional shifts. From the hormonal adjustments triggering heightened empathy to the increased sense of responsibility and fulfillment, we uncovered the multifaceted nature of this transformative experience.

Key insights from this chapter emphasize how important it is to understand and prepare for the challenges and joys of fatherhood. We emphasized the significance of mental health awareness and seeking support when needed to navigate the inevitable obstacles that arise.

As we transition to the next chapter, "Strategize with Your Partner," it's clear that effective communication and collaboration are paramount in navigating the complexities of parenthood. Let's recognize the value of joining forces with our significant other to develop practical parenting strategies together without relying on cliches. Together, we can face the upcoming challenges and cherish the moments of joy that await us on this shared journey.

Instruction Manual for First-Time Dads

Chapter 6

Strategize With Your Partner

It's a typical day in the life of a working dad, and yours truly is trying to conquer the towering mountain of tasks looming on my desk. Emails are piling up faster than I can hit "reply," and meetings seem to multiply like rabbits. Meanwhile, my phone lights up like a Christmas tree with messages from home, a gentle reminder of my real-life juggling act. Amidst this chaos, I steal a moment to gaze at a cherished family photo, where laughter and love leap out from the frame, reminding me of the beautiful chaos awaiting me after work. In moments like these, I realize the delicate balance I strive to maintain, the tightrope walk between career aspirations and cuddles with my little ones. In this chapter, we're diving headfirst into the whirlwind of balancing work and family life. From deciphering the art of effective communication to crafting strategic plans with your partner, join me on this journey as we navigate the wild terrain of parenthood together. Get ready to discover the challenges, embrace the importance of open dialogue, and master strategizing with your partner. It's time to turn the chaos into a symphony of success, one harmonious note at a time.

Instruction Manual for First-Time Dads

Change Can Be Challenging

Experiencing any form of change can feel like surfing unpredictable waves, especially when embracing fatherhood's twists and turns. Yet, amidst the whirlwind of diapers and sleepless nights, remember this: your involvement as a dad is nothing short of pivotal. You shape your child's emotional landscape, laying the foundation for their well-being and resilience. Your affectionate presence fosters cognitive growth and social aptitude, nurturing a sense of security and confidence that sets the stage for a lifetime of flourishing relationships. Whether you're guiding your daughter through life's challenges or showing your son the ropes of manhood, your influence ripples far beyond the confines of the home.

That said, it's essential to recognize the challenges ahead. From balancing the demands of work and financial responsibilities to navigating the complexities of learning to be a dad, each hurdle presents a unique opportunity for growth and adaptation. Additionally, the lack of support from the workplace and the need to maintain a strong and thriving marital bond amidst the chaos of parenthood can further add to the adventure.

Don't forget about other challenges, like the ups and downs of having a baby, decisions about parenting, intimate relationships, or communication. It all can be a bit overwhelming. But when you start learning what you can expect, the better prepared you will become.

Work and Financial Responsibilities

Balancing work and financial responsibilities feels like a tightrope, doesn't it? Take Jake, a devoted father of two who works long hours to provide for his family. He loves his job but is also acutely aware of the precious moments slipping by with his kids. The pressure can be overwhelming when he's torn between staying late at the office for a crucial project or making it home in time for his daughter's soccer game. But Jake knows that finding that delicate balance is essential for his family's well-being. By prioritizing quality time with his loved ones and setting boundaries at work, he's learning to navigate the tricky terrain of work-life balance one step at a time (*Top Challenges Every Dad Face*, 2023).

Lack of Support From the Workplace

The lack of support from the workplace can feel like hitting a brick wall, especially for dads like Mark, who want to be actively involved in their children's lives. When his company announced a new policy that discouraged employees from taking parental leave, Mark felt torn. He wanted to be there for his wife during the birth of their second child, but he also feared the repercussions of taking time off work. Would his colleagues see him as less committed? Would his boss pass him over for that promotion he'd been eyeing? It was a tough decision, but Mark knew his family came first. By advocating for himself and pushing for change within his company, he's paving the way for a more supportive workplace culture for fathers everywhere (Allied Health, 2023).

Learning How to Be a Dad

Learning how to dad is an experience filled with unexpected twists and turns. Just ask Tom. As a first-time father, he was eager to dive into the role headfirst, armed with all the parenting books and YouTube tutorials he could find. But when his newborn daughter arrived, he quickly realized that there was no manual for fatherhood—from mastering the art of swaddling to soothing late-night cries, every day brought a new challenge. But Tom embraced the journey with open arms, learning from each experience and cherishing the precious moments he shared with his daughter. There were sleepless nights and diaper disasters along the way, but seeing her smile made it all worth it! (*Top Challenges Every Dad Face*, 2023).

Strengthening the Marital Bond

Strengthening the marital bond is like tending to a garden. It requires time, effort, and plenty of love. Just ask Mike and Sarah, who found themselves navigating the rocky terrain of parenthood after the birth of their twins. With two demanding jobs and two demanding infants, they faced a whole lot of challenges within their relationship. They struggled to find time for each other amidst the chaos of diaper changes and midnight feedings. But instead of letting parenthood drive them apart, Mike and Sarah consciously prioritized their relationship. They carved out date nights, took turns giving each other much-needed breaks, and never forgot to say "I love you" at the end of a long day. By nurturing their bond with open communication and unwavering support, they weathered the storm of parenthood together, emerging stronger and more connected than ever before (Allied Health, 2023).

Relationship Ups and Downs

I've mentioned it once, and I'll mention it again, having a baby is a rollercoaster ride, where the highs are higher than you could ever imagine, and the lows can leave you feel like you're free-falling. For many new parents like you, the transition to parenthood can bring about a whirlwind of emotions, from sheer joy to overwhelming exhaustion. Take a moment to catch your breath and acknowledge that feeling a little lost in chaos is okay. After all, you're navigating uncharted territory together with your partner, and it's natural for tensions to run high as you both adjust to your new roles. Every moment brings its own set of challenges and triumphs, from the plentiful diaper changes to the disastrous lack of sleep. But remember, you're in this together. When you practice patience and do everything with unconditional love, you'll weather the storm and emerge stronger than ever.

Decisions About Parenting After Childbirth

Next, we have the age-old question, "Who's the boss?" When it comes to parenting after childbirth, it's not uncommon for couples to find themselves at odds over the best way to raise their little bundle of joy. From breastfeeding vs. bottle-feeding to co-sleeping vs. sleep training, the options seem endless, and opinions can clash. But here's the thing: a one-size-fits-all parenting approach doesn't exist. So, instead of getting caught up in who's right and who's wrong, try to embrace your differences and find common ground (*How to Be a Parenting Team*, 2023). Remember, you both have the same goal: raising a happy, healthy baby, and it takes a team effort.

Physical Relationships

Of course, we must think about post-baby intimacy, or lack thereof. Between sleepless nights, hormonal fluctuations, and the sheer exhaustion of caring for a newborn, the last thing on your mind may be getting frisky between the sheets. That's perfectly okay. Parenthood is a marathon, not a sprint; there's no rush to jump back into the bedroom before you're ready. Communication is key here, folks. Be honest with your partner about what you need and desire physically, and don't be afraid to take things slow. Whether cuddling on the couch or stealing a kiss in the kitchen, find ways to connect that feel comfortable for both of you. Remember, there's no "right" time to get back in the saddle. Trust your instincts and do what feels right for you (*Being a New Parent: Sex after Pregnancy*, 2022).

Relationships With Others

Parenthood has a funny way of shining a spotlight on your relationships with friends and family. Some may offer support and guidance, while others may seem to fade into the background. It's essential to recognize that everyone's journey is different; not everyone will understand or agree with your parenting choices. Instead of getting bogged down by other people's opinions, focus on what's best for your family.

Surround yourself with a support system of friends and family who lift you and cheer you on, and don't be afraid to lean on them when times get tough (*Changes in Your Relationships After Having a Baby*, 2019). For those friends who don't quite understand this new phase of your life, give them time. They might come around, or your paths together might come to an end. That's okay, too. Not every relationship is meant to last forever.

Role of Communication When Navigating Needs and Changes

Communication bonds relationships, especially during times of change and uncertainty. Throughout the ups and downs of parenthood, open and honest communication with your partner is more important than ever. I've said it a few times already, but that's because it's such a crucial part of parenthood. Listen to each other's needs, concerns, and frustrations. Then, find ways to meet both of your needs, whether through compromise or creative solutions. Remember, you're a team, and the only way to tackle the challenges of parenthood is by supporting each other every step of the way.

Tips to Improve Communication

You can improve communication with your partner in a few ways. Start by making time for regular check-ins, where you can discuss your feelings, share your triumphs and struggles, and brainstorm solutions together. When you express your thoughts and feelings, be sure to use "I" statements without placing blame on your partner. Of course, active listening is also key. As you listen to your partner, make eye contact, ask genuine questions, and show interest, understanding, and empathy (*Communicating with Your Partner in the Perinatal Period*, n.d.). Parenthood may be tough, but with a little patience, understanding, and a whole lot of love, you and your partner can overcome any obstacle that comes your way.

Strategize With Your Partner

Balancing the responsibilities of parenthood with the demands of a career can feel overwhelming. Still, with careful planning and teamwork, you and your partner can find a harmonious work-life balance. Here are several strategies to help you navigate this journey together (Novak, 2020):

1. **Establish a family calendar:** Create a centralized calendar to record each family member's schedules, appointments, and commitments. It helps both you and your partner stay organized and informed about each other's availability and childcare responsibilities. For example, you can link your Google Calendars or family organizer apps for easy access and updates.
2. **Choose quality childcare:** Research and select options that align with your values and provide a nurturing environment for your little one. Whether it's a daycare center, a nanny, or a family member, ensure that your child is in safe and reliable hands while you're at work.
3. **Divide and conquer:** Share parenting responsibilities with your partner and create a fair division of tasks at home. Coordinate schedules, childcare arrangements, and household chores to ensure you contribute equally to family life.
4. **Have a backup plan:** Prepare for unexpected situations by having a backup babysitter or family member who can assist when needed. It provides

peace of mind, knowing you have support in case your primary childcare arrangement falls through or emergencies arise.

5. **Streamline your mornings:** Make your morning routines easier by preparing as much as possible the previous night. For instance, pack lunches, lay out clothes, and organize essentials like diaper bags to minimize last-minute chaos. Establishing a consistent morning routine reduces stress and starts your day in a more organized, triumphant way.

6. **Communicate with your employer:** Maintain open communication about your childcare needs and explore flexible work arrangements. Discuss options for remote work, flexible hours, or parental leave to accommodate your family responsibilities while meeting professional obligations.

7. **Prioritize self-care:** Be sure to make time for yourself to recharge and rejuvenate. Whether exercising, meditating, or pursuing hobbies, prioritize activities that promote your well-being. Remember, the better you care for yourself, the better parent and partner you can become.

8. **Stay connected with each other:** Nurture your relationship with your partner by actively planning quality time together. For example, schedule weekly date nights to reconnect and strengthen your bond amidst the demands of parenthood and work.

9. **Set manageable expectations:** Accept that achieving a perfect balance between work and parenthood is unrealistic. Embrace imperfection

and focus on doing your best rather than striving for perfection. Adjust your expectations based on your evolving circumstances and be flexible amid the chaos.

10. **Seek support networks:** Build a support network of fellow dads, family, and friends who understand what type of challenge you're facing. That way, you engage with people who'll help you see the joys of parenthood and conquer the complexities that come with it.

By implementing these strategies and prioritizing open communication, teamwork, and self-care, you and your partner can successfully navigate balancing work and parenthood while fostering a happy and fulfilling family life. Remember to celebrate the milestones, cherish the moments together, and lean on each other for support during both the challenging and rewarding times ahead.

As we conclude this chapter, it's clear that you and your partner's road ahead is as dynamic as it is rewarding. From navigating the delicate dance of work and family life to strengthening the bonds of partnership amidst the chaos of parenthood, each chapter brings its own set of hurdles and victories. As we turn the page to our next chapter, "Personal Time," we delve into the importance of carving out moments of respite amidst the whirlwind of responsibilities.

Just as a tightrope walker must find balance amidst the dizzying heights, so must we find equilibrium between our roles as parents, partners, and individuals. In "Personal Time," we'll explore strategies for reclaiming precious moments of self-care and rejuvenation amidst the demands of daily life. From establishing boundaries and prioritizing self-care to nurturing hobbies and interests outside of parental duties, we'll uncover the power of personal time to foster resilience and well-being.

Remember to celebrate the small victories and prioritize moments of rest and rejuvenation along the way. After all, in the symphony of parenthood, every note, both harmonious and discordant, contributes to the beautiful melody of family life.

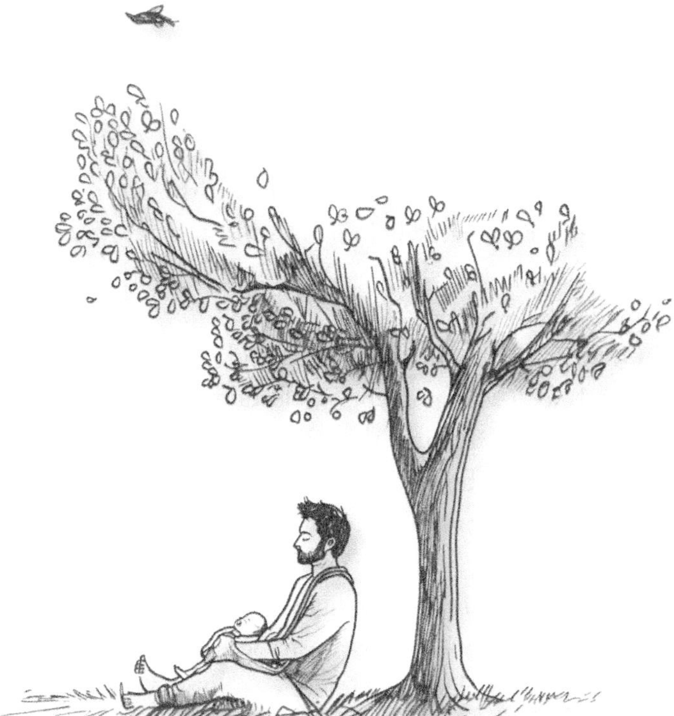

Chapter 7

Personal Time

As a first-time dad, I found the whirlwind of parenthood exhilarating and overwhelming. Amidst the joyous chaos of diaper changes and sleepless nights, I stumbled upon a vital lesson. The importance of personal time.

One evening, amidst the cries and coos of our newborn, I realized I needed a moment of solitude. Stepping out into the quiet night and feeling the cool air for myself amidst the demands of fatherhood.

In those solitary moments, I found solace and renewed energy away from the hustle and bustle of parenthood. It struck me then, like a beam of moonlight cutting through the darkness, that nurturing my well-being wasn't selfish, it was essential.

Through this chapter, I invite you into my journey, where I share practical insights intertwined with personal anecdotes. From brief walks to quiet reflections, I discovered that carving out personal time isn't just a luxury, it's a necessity.

To all the first-time dads out there, amidst the diaper changes and midnight feedings, remember to prioritize self-care. Embrace those fleeting moments of solitude, for they are the cornerstone of resilience in the beautiful chaos of fatherhood.

You Need Alone Time, Too!

Let's explore why self-care isn't just a fancy term tossed around by wellness gurus. It's your secret weapon for thriving in the fatherhood adventure. You, a rookie dad, are diving headfirst into the chaos of diapers, late-night feedings, and adorable baby giggles. You're a superhero in disguise, but even superheroes need a break sometimes. Your first few weeks into fatherhood might mean you ignore self-care, soldier on, and rely on caffeine and sheer determination to fuel your daily actions. As days turn into weeks, exhaustion creeps in, turning your once sunny disposition into a cloud of stress and fatigue.

Your relationships feel the strain, your health takes a hit, and suddenly, being a super dad doesn't feel so super anymore. However, by embracing self-care, you recharge your batteries, boost your mood, and show up as the best dad version of yourself. Cape optional. Take some time to prioritize self-care, not because it is a luxury but because it is a lifeline to navigate fatherhood with grace, energy, and maybe even a few extra hours of sleep.

Many first-time dads and moms often neglect self-care amidst the whirlwind of parenthood. It isn't a phenomenon exclusive to a few, it's an experience every dad undergoes. Like an unwelcome guest, guilt settles in, convincing parents that prioritizing themselves is synonymous with neglecting their responsibilities. Time slips away under responsibilities in both professional and parental capacities. Financial strains only amplify the pressure, whispering that indulging in self-care is a luxury they can not afford. Social expectations compound these feelings, perpetuating the myth that parents must martyr themselves for the sake of their children. As a result, self-care falls by the wayside, buried beneath a mountain of parental duties.

I get it. Putting your baby's and family's needs above your own is easy. But it's really important to prioritize it. And if you're still a bit unsure, let's look at the different benefits self-care can have for you (Castro, 2023):

- **Improved mental health:** You tackle diaper duty with a smile, shrug off sleepless nights like a champ, and face those baby tantrums with zen-like calmness. How? Because self-care gives your mental health the TLC it deserves. It turns stress into child's play.
- **Enhanced physical health:** Say goodbye to the dad-bod blues! With a dash of exercise, a sprinkle of nutritious meals, and a dollop of quality shut-eye, you'll power through playtime marathons and keep up with your little one's boundless energy.
- **Increased productivity:** Who needs a cape when you've got self-care? Carving out time for yourself will supercharge your productivity levels, allowing you to smash through your to-do list with ease and efficiency.
- **Better relationships**: Want to be the hero in your family's story? Start by investing in yourself! By nurturing your well-being, you'll show up as the best version of yourself, deepening connections and creating precious memories with your loved ones.
- **Stress reduction:** Let's face it, parenthood can be a wild rollercoaster ride. But with self-care as

your trusted sidekick, you'll breeze through the twists and turns with ease while keeping stress levels in check and embracing each moment with a smile.
- **Role modeling:** As your mini-me looks up to you with wide-eyed wonder, you have the power to be their ultimate role model. By prioritizing self-care, you're not just setting an example—you're laying the groundwork for them to prioritize their own self-love and self-care habits.

Now that you're armed with the incredible benefits of self-care, isn't it time you stopped neglecting yourself and started prioritizing your well-being? After all, you're setting the stage for a happier, healthier family life.

If you're wondering how to implement self-care as a priority in your life, here are a few tips to consider:

- **Schedule "me time":** Block out dedicated time in your calendar for self-care activities, whether it's hitting the gym, indulging in a hobby, or simply unwinding with a good book. Like other important appointments, treat your self-care as a non-negotiable—you wouldn't cancel on your boss, so why cancel yourself?
- **Delegate and share responsibilities:** You don't have to be a one-man show! Ask for help from your partner, family, or friends to get a bit of the load off your shoulders. Whether splitting household chores, taking turns with nighttime feedings, or arranging playdates for your little one, sharing responsibilities will free up precious time for self-care.

- **Set boundaries:** You can decline commitments that don't align with your priorities. Whether it's turning down extra work projects, declining social invitations, or setting limits on screen time, setting boundaries will help you reclaim control of your time and energy.
- **Practice self-compassion:** Kindness to yourself, especially on those tough parenting days, is truly important. Remember, you're doing the best you can, and it's okay to ask for help or take a break when you need it.
- **Find joy in everyday moments:** Taking care of yourself doesn't have to be grandiose gestures or take up all your time. Look for opportunities to infuse joy into your daily routine, whether savoring your morning coffee, taking a mindful walk in nature, or sharing a laugh with your little one.
- **Stay connected:** Social connections are a wonderful way to boost your well-being. While it might be challenging, schedule time to spend with family, friends, or fellow dads who understand the joys and challenges of fatherhood. Whether it's a weekly meet-up or a quick phone call, staying connected will help you feel supported and valued.

By incorporating these self-care strategies into your daily life, you'll become a happier, healthier dad and set a positive example for your little one.

Creating and Following a Self-Care Routine

You can choose between different self-care options. And it's best to choose whichever type will bring you more joy or combine them all. They include the following:

- **Emotional self-care** involves nurturing your inner feelings and thoughts, creating a sense of balance and resilience. It can include taking time for self-reflection, practicing positive self-talk, or enjoying a weekly bubble bath to unwind and destress.
- **Physical self-care** is to maintain and enhance your physical health and well-being. Prioritizing regular exercise that you enjoy, getting enough sleep each night, and fueling your body with nourishing foods are all examples of physical self-care.
- **Spiritual self-care** involves nourishing your spirit. It can be achieved through spending time in nature, practicing meditation or mindfulness, or engaging in acts of kindness and gratitude.
- **Social self-care** emphasizes nurturing and maintaining healthy relationships with others. Scheduling regular coffee dates or phone calls with friends, joining a community group or club, and volunteering in your local community are all ways to practice social self-care.
- **Intellectual self-care** focuses on stimulating your mind and expanding your knowledge and skills. Reading books or articles on topics that interest you, taking up a new hobby, learning a new

skill, and engaging in stimulating conversations with others are all examples of intellectual self-care.
- **Environmental self-care** is when you spend time creating a supportive and nurturing environment that promotes your well-being. It can include decluttering and organizing your living space, spending time in nature, or surrounding yourself with positive and uplifting people.

As you can see, self-care isn't about fancy spa days or pricey indulgences. It's about the little moments that bring you joy and peace. Whether savoring your morning shower or taking a moment to appreciate the beauty around you, self-care is personal and unique to you. Indulge in activities that make you feel alive and rejuvenated without worrying about the price tag. Remember, it's often the free things in life that can bring more joy and fulfillment than the materialistic.

Starting a self-care routine is like planting seeds of love and nourishment. Begin by choosing one small act of self-care and making it part of your daily routine. Maybe it's a morning stretch or a few minutes of deep breathing. Practice it consistently for a week and notice how it makes you feel. As you build momentum, add more self-care practices that resonate with you.

With that said, here are five steps you can take to create and get into a self-care routine (Lawler, 2022):

1. **Identify your sources of joy:** Start by exploring activities or experiences that bring you happiness and relaxation. Whether it's the scent of fresh flowers, a warm cup of tea, or your favorite

playlist, jot down anything that lifts your spirits and makes you feel centered.
2. **Incorporate joyful moments:** Brainstorm ways to weave these sources of joy into your daily life. It could be as simple as surrounding yourself with comforting scents or setting aside time each day for a cherished hobby. Start small and gradually integrate these moments into your routine.
3. **Set achievable goals:** Define realistic goals for practicing self-care daily. Whether allocating a few minutes for mindfulness meditation or unplugging from screens during meal times, set clear objectives that you can track and measure. As you accomplish each goal, challenge yourself to level up and embrace more enriching self-care practices.
4. **Seek support:** Share your self-care journey with supportive friends or family members with similar interests. Having a support system can help you stay accountable and motivated while also providing encouragement and inspiration along the way.
5. **Adapt and evolve:** Self-care won't always look the same for you. It's a process that needs constant evaluation and adaptation over time. Be open-minded about trying different self-care practices and modifying your routine as your needs evolve. Remember, it's okay to embrace trial and error as you discover what truly nurtures your well-being.

Incorporating self-care doesn't have to be complicated. Start small, divide it into manageable actions, and gradually elaborate on your routine as you find what works best for you. Whether enjoying a quiet moment with a good book or savoring a homemade meal, prioritize activities that replenish your energy and nurture your soul.

It's Okay to Ask for Help

Like moms, dads need a supportive community to lean on during those uncertain moments. Here's why reaching out for support is not only okay but essential for dads:

When Nigel Clarke, author and TV presenter, became a father, he initially believed he didn't need support. However, he soon realized the importance of having a community of fellow fathers to share experiences. Parenting can be daunting, and interacting with other dads you can relate to can provide invaluable reassurance and guidance.

Dad groups offer a safe space for fathers to discuss their experiences, seek advice, and form meaningful connections with like-minded individuals. Whether it's sharing stories, exchanging parenting tips, or simply finding solidarity in shared challenges, these groups play a crucial role in supporting dads through their parenting journey. Here are a few more benefits of engaging in dad communities (*Why Dads Need Support Too!*, 2023):

- **Confidence-building:** Dad groups provide a platform for fathers to build confidence in their parenting abilities. By sharing insights and learning from others, dads can gain the reassurance they need to navigate the ups and downs of fatherhood.
- **Emotional support:** Parenting can be emotionally taxing, and having a supportive community to turn to can alleviate feelings of

isolation and stress. Dad groups offer a space where fathers can express their concerns, share their triumphs, and find comfort in knowing they're not alone.

- **Mental well-being:** Dads' mental health is often overlooked, but it's just as important as moms'. One thing that can positively impact your well-being is to engage in dad communities. Within these groups, you'll feel a sense of belonging and, ultimately, your mental state. By normalizing conversations around mental health, these groups empower dads to prioritize self-care and seek support when needed.
- **Modern parenting:** Dad's roles in parenting have evolved significantly in recent years, with more fathers actively involved in childcare and household responsibilities. Dad groups embrace this shift by celebrating hands-on fatherhood and providing resources tailored to modern dads' needs.

Don't be shy about looking for communities to become a necessary part of your life. For dads seeking support and camaraderie, numerous online platforms and resources cater specifically to fathers:

- **City Dads Group:** Connect with dads in your city through meet-ups and events.
- **The Dad Gang:** Join a community of Black fathers changing perceptions of fatherhood.
- **Fatherly:** Get expert advice on fatherhood, from pregnancy to parenting teens.
- **DadVerb:** Watch relatable videos covering various dad-related topics.

- **Dope Black Dads:** Engage in a safe space for Black fathers to share experiences.
- **Tinyhood Circle:** Join a virtual community offering discussions and events.
- **Mama meet-ups by MOPS:** Connect with moms worldwide for support and socializing.
- **Peanut:** Access a social media app specifically for moms to foster friendships.
- **Fatherhood.org:** Find resources for responsible fatherhood, including e-books and webinars.
- **Fathers.com:** Read quick insights about fatherhood and connect with other dads.
- **Wilderdad:** Explore outdoor adventures and parenting tips for stronger families.
- **Fatherhood.gov:** Access educational resources and events for fathers.
- **Special Advantage:** Join a community for special needs families that offers coaching and support.
- **National Parent Helpline:** Find local support groups and resources for family needs.

Remember, you're not weak if you ask for help. Instead, it's a testament to your commitment to being your best dad. Don't hesitate to reach out and connect with other fathers who can offer guidance, encouragement, and a listening ear along the way.

In our exploration of self-care for first-time dads, we've uncovered the vital importance of nurturing our own well-being amidst the beautiful chaos of fatherhood. From prioritizing personal time to embracing self-care practices, we've delved into the transformative benefits of investing in ourselves. As we turn the page to the next chapter, "Partner Time," let's

Instruction Manual for First-Time Dads

dig deeper into the dynamics of shared responsibilities and the power of fostering connections with our partners. Together, we'll learn to create a balance between the joys and challenges of parenting, strengthening our bonds as co-pilots on this exhilarating journey.

Chapter 8

Partner Time

WELCOME to the next chapter of our fatherhood adventure, where we dive into the world of supporting our partners through the ups and downs of postpartum life. Did you know that about 1 in 10 women experience postpartum depression after they give birth? Some studies even suggest it's as high as 1 in 7 (Carberg, 2023). It's like discovering a hidden level in the game of parenthood, one that requires extra care, attention, and understanding.

Postpartum depression typically sticks around for about 3 to 6 months, but the duration can differ depending on each mom's unique journey. Here's the kicker: Almost half of the moms dealing with it aren't diagnosed by healthcare professionals. That's where we come in, armed with love, empathy, and maybe a superhero cape.

As rookie dads, it's our job to be the Robin to our partners' Batman, supporting them through every twist and turn. In this chapter, we'll explore how to recognize the signs, offer a shoulder to lean on, and keep the flame of romance burning— even when diapers and midnight feedings threaten to dim the mood. So grab your partner's hand, and let's navigate this adventure together with laughter, love, and much understanding.

Understanding Postpartum Depression

Postpartum depression (PPD) isn't just feeling a bit down after giving birth—it's like a storm of emotions, both physical and emotional, that can hit some women within four weeks of delivery. It's a bit like major depression but with a post-baby twist. The severity and duration of these depressive episodes are what set it apart. Postpartum depression isn't just about hormones taking a nosedive post-delivery. While that's part of it, the social and psychological changes that come with becoming a new mom also play a significant role. Imagine a whirlwind of emotions where feelings of sadness, despair, and anxiety mingle with the sheer joy and exhaustion of caring for a newborn. Dads aren't left untouched by this, either. Research shows that about 1 in 10 new fathers experience depression during their child's first year (Bruce, 2022). You and your partner can navigate these challenges with understanding and support. It might even help you get closer and set the stage for a brighter, happier family.

Postpartum Depression Signs and Symptoms

Spotting the signs of postpartum depression can be tricky—they often blend in with the usual challenges of new motherhood. Things like trouble sleeping, appetite changes, fatigue, and mood swings are common. However, when these symptoms stick around and are accompanied by feelings of worthlessness, hopelessness, and even thoughts of harming oneself or the baby, it's time to seek help.

Symptoms of postpartum depression can include (Bruce, 2022):

- Difficulties sleeping
- Changes in appetite
- Extreme fatigue
- Decreased libido
- Constant mood changes

In some cases, postpartum depression can manifest as obsessive-compulsive disorder (OCD) or panic disorder, adding another layer of complexity to the mix.

Postpartum Depression Causes and Risk Factors

Postpartum depression isn't a reflection of anything you did wrong! It's a complex interplay of factors that range from hormonal shifts and lack of sleep to anxiety and self-image concerns that contribute to its onset.

Factors that can increase a mother's chances of getting postpartum depression include the following (Bruce, 2022):

- A history of depression
- Age at the time of pregnancy
- Ambivalence about pregnancy
- Family history of mood disorders
- Stressful life events

A history of depression, age, ambivalence about pregnancy, family history, and stressful life events are just some of the factors that can increase the likelihood of postpartum depression. And let's not forget the physical toll like hormonal fluctuations, sleep deprivation, and the overwhelming responsibilities of caring for a newborn can all take their toll on a new mom's mental health.

Types of Postpartum Depression

Postpartum mood changes come in various forms, from the

fleeting "baby blues" to the more severe postpartum depression and postpartum psychosis. We've all heard of the baby blues. They're like those passing clouds in the sky that disappear independently, typically within a few weeks. Postpartum depression, on the other hand, is a bit more persistent—it's like an uninvited guest who stays way longer than you'd like. Don't worry, with some TLC and professional support, it's manageable. And then there's postpartum psychosis, extremely rare but serious, needing immediate attention like a superhero swooping in to save the day.

Types of postpartum depression include the following (Bruce, 2022):

- **Baby blues:** Like a passing cloud, disappearing within a few weeks.
- **Postpartum depression:** The uninvited guest who overstays their welcome but is manageable with support.
- **Postpartum psychosis:** Super severe but rare, needing immediate attention like a superhero.

Understanding these types allows you to better navigate the emotional landscape of your partner's transition into motherhood. So, whether it's passing about the baby blues or a more persistent struggle with postpartum depression, knowing the signs and seeking assistance can be the beacon of light guiding a new mom toward healing and well-being.

Postpartum Depression Treatment

When it comes to treating postpartum depression (PPD), seeking professional help is key. The support can come from various sources, like your prenatal care provider, primary care provider, or a mental health professional. These people are educated and will get your partner the right treatment options she needs, which include support groups, counseling, or even medication, depending on how severe the condition is (*Postpartum Depression*, 2019). Remember, the sooner your partner gets help, the sooner she can start feeling like herself again.

Postpartum Depression Complications

Untreated postpartum depression can have ripple effects, affecting not just the mom but the entire family. From weakening the bond between mom and baby to increasing the risk of depression in the future, the consequences can be far-reaching. Let's not forget about the dad. When mom is struggling, dads can feel the impact too, with research showing they're more likely to experience depression as well. Plus, children of moms with postpartum depression may face challenges with sleeping, eating, and language development. That's why addressing PPD head-on and seeking the necessary support is crucial.

Postpartum Depression Prevention

While it may not always be possible to prevent postpartum depression entirely, there are steps you can take to lower the risk. For example, if your partner has a history of depression, it's a good idea to go for counseling during pregnancy as a preventative measure. Additionally, maintaining a healthy lifestyle, staying connected with loved ones, and reducing stress wherever possible can all contribute to overall well-being. Remember, taking care of mom's mental health is a team effort, so don't hesitate to offer your support every step of the way (*Postpartum Depression*, 2019).

Here are ten ways dads can support their partners through postpartum depression (Bruce, 2022):

- Listen to your partner's feelings without judgment and with pure interest.

- Motivate her and help her get professional help.
- Take on extra household responsibilities to ease her burden.
- Offer reassurance and emotional support.
- Plan small outings or activities to boost her mood.
- Help facilitate connections with friends and family.
- Encourage her to take care of herself, like exercising or relaxing.
- Be patient while she navigates through her emotions, and try to understand their impact on her.
- Learn as much as you can about postpartum depression so you can understand her experience better.
- Above all, tell her she can count on your love and support.

Your unwavering support can make a significant difference in helping your partner overcome postpartum depression and emerge stronger together as a family.

Keeping the Fire Alive

As a first-time dad, I can relate to the anticipation and uncertainty surrounding postpartum intimacy. After our baby's arrival, we eagerly awaited the six-week mark recommended by healthcare professionals. However, we soon realized that my partner's body needed more time to heal. It took several months before we felt comfortable fully embracing intimacy again, prioritizing open communication and patience. Similarly, my partner's menstrual cycle returned gradually several months after childbirth. These experiences taught us how important patience, understanding, and support for each other are throughout the postpartum period's challenges. Remember, every couple's experience is unique, so trust in each other and your journey together.

A common concern most couples have post-birth is regarding sex. And it's no wonder. The mom just went through a pretty traumatic experience bringing your little one into this world. Chances are that she won't be up for sex immediately. You and your partner might notice a shift in your bedroom dynamics after your bundle of joy arrives. You have less time, feel more exhausted, and your partner experiences a whole lot of hormonal changes that can make getting frisky a bit tricky. It's like trying to schedule a romantic dinner date when your calendar's full of diaper changes and sleepless nights.

It's common for the birthing mom to feel like her libido took a vacation post-baby. Don't worry! It will make a triumphant comeback soon. Some moms even find themselves feeling all kinds of sensual while breastfeeding, thanks to our buddy oxytocin (Ruddy, 2023). If you're not feeling the heat just yet, don't sweat it. It's like waiting for your favorite TV show to return from hiatus. It will be worth the wait!

Let's talk about post-baby bodies. Your partner's been through a lot, so it's crucial to let her take the lead when getting back in the saddle. Stitches, tears, or just feeling a bit off? No problem. Take it slow, use some lube if needed, and remember, it's all about finding your groove again. As you wait for that flame to reignite, don't underestimate how a simple cuddle session can affect intimacy.

When you're both finally ready for sex, it's necessary to be on the same page about contraception. After childbirth, a woman's body can surprise you by gearing up for another baby sooner than you might think. Ovulation can kick back into gear just weeks after giving birth, putting the baby-making machinery back in motion (Ruddy, 2023). That's where contraception steps in as your trusty sidekick, providing peace of mind and ensuring you're not in for a surprise sequel before you're ready. If you don't want another baby just yet, talk to your doctor to explore your options and find the best fit for your family planning needs.

Of course, you know that sex isn't just about growing your family. It's about getting closer to your partner again. However, after childbirth, things might feel a tad different down there. Whether your partner delivered naturally or via C-section, she might experience discomfort or pain during intimacy. Blame those hormonal shifts for making things a bit dry and less elastic (Ruddy, 2023). And if she's breastfeeding, get ready for a sneak peek into the world of menopause, —hot flashes and all. Don't worry, even C-section parents can feel a little postpartum discomfort. Healing takes time, so take it easy.

Now, onto one last not-so-sexy topic before I give you some tips to improve your intimacy. Constipation. Yes, you heard it right, constipation can be a real buzzkill for bedroom fun. After childbirth, it's common for moms to experience discomfort, straining, and hard stools. Factors like medication, soreness, and changes in routine contribute to this not-so-glamorous issue. But staying hydrated, eating fiber-rich foods, and engaging in gentle exercise can help mom get things moving smoothly again. And if the discomfort persists, don't hesitate to call your doctor for tips and guidance. Remember, a happy tummy makes for happier times in the bedroom!

With all those little nuggets to help you understand intimacy after having a baby, let's get into some tips on how you can keep the spark alive (McConville, 2023):

- **Rekindle romance:** Take a break from dad duties and spend quality time with your partner. Hire a babysitter and revisit your favorite pre-baby activities. Whether it's a romantic dinner at your go-to spot or a spontaneous adventure, reconnecting sans baby can reignite that spark.
- **Ease into it:** Postpartum sex can be daunting, but intimacy comes in many forms. Enjoy tender moments together, like snuggling together or holding hands in those in-between moments you have to yourselves. Start small with gestures like a gentle massage or a loving embrace to ease back into physical closeness.
- **Embrace creativity:** Parenthood is full of surprises, so get creative with your intimacy. Find unique places for romance, like a cozy corner of the house or a quick rendezvous during nap time. Embrace spontaneity and keep the excitement alive, whether stealing kisses in the kitchen or sneaking away for a private moment.
- **Support your partner:** Your partner's body has been through a lot, so offer your unwavering support and understanding. Encourage open communication about post-baby changes and reassure your partner of your love and attraction.
- **Make time for love:** Parenthood can be exhausting, but don't let it overshadow your intimacy. Keep the passion alive with thoughtful gestures, like sending flirty texts or planning surprise date nights. Even amidst the chaos of parenting, make your relationship a priority and spend much-needed time together.

Instruction Manual for First-Time Dads

- **Prioritize self-care:** Take care of yourself mentally and physically to be the best partner and parent you can be. Find moments to recharge, whether going on walks or working on a hobby you love. Communicate your needs with your partner and support each other in prioritizing self-care.
- **Communicate openly:** Be open with your partner about your concerns and desires. Have regular check-ins where you both can share what you think and feel without being judged. From discussing your favorite memories as a couple to expressing your needs in the bedroom, honest communication strengthens your bond.
- **Team up:** Parenthood is a team effort, so work alongside your partner. Show appreciation for each other's efforts and celebrate your mutual successes. Whether it's sharing parenting duties or cheering each other on during late-night feedings, being a united front strengthens your relationship and builds a strong foundation for your family.

Remember, Dad, you play a crucial role in keeping your relationship's love and desire alive. Cherish these moments with your growing family, and embrace the journey together.

Congratulations, Dad! You've reached the end of this incredible journey through first-time fatherhood. Reflecting on each chapter, you've gained invaluable insights and tools to navigate this new chapter of your life with confidence and grace.

From preparing for your baby's arrival to understanding their needs and milestones, you've equipped yourself with the knowledge and skills to be a hands-on and supportive dad. You've learned the importance of bonding with your newborn, feeding them with care, and tracking their development every step of the way.

As you continue this adventure, remember the importance of caring for yourself and communicating openly with your partner. Balancing personal and professional life as a parent may present challenges, but you can overcome any obstacle with strategic planning and teamwork.

Above all, never underestimate the power of your love and support for your partner. By being there for them every step of the way, you strengthen your bond as a couple and create a nurturing environment for your family to thrive.

Moving forward, know that you are an excellent dad and partner. Embrace the lessons you've learned from this book and trust your ability to navigate fatherhood with confidence, compassion, and love.

Afterword

Congratulations, fellow dad, on finishing this book! As you reflect on the chapters you've explored, remember that each step has been a building block in the foundation of your role as a father. From the early preparations for your newborn to the ongoing support for your partner, you've embraced the challenges and joys of parenthood with courage and determination.

In Chapter 1, you discovered the importance of readiness and preparation for your newborn's arrival. From setting up the nursery to ensuring your home is baby-proof, you took proactive steps to create a safe and welcoming environment for your little one. These preparations laid the groundwork for a smooth transition into fatherhood, allowing you to focus on bonding with and nurturing your newborn from the moment they arrived.

Chapter 2 delved into the profound bond between parent and child, emphasizing the importance of connection and attachment in those early days. You've learned how to nurture a deep and lasting bond with your baby by having skin-to-skin contact, looking into your baby's eyes, and caring for them

Afterword

responsively. These moments of closeness strengthened your relationship and became the cornerstone for your little one's emotional development and well-being.

As you explored the nuances of feeding in Chapter 3, you navigated the complexities of breastfeeding and bottle-feeding with confidence and compassion. By understanding your baby's cues and needs, you provided nourishment and comfort in equal measure, fostering a healthy feeding relationship that would sustain your child in the months and years to come. With this knowledge, you're also able to support your partner throughout every feeding session.

Chapter 4 brought a deeper understanding of your baby's development, from those early milestones to ongoing growth and discovery. By tracking your child's progress and celebrating their achievements, you embraced each stage of development with wonder and joy, recognizing the unique gifts and talents they bring to the world.

In Chapter 5, you dug deeper into personal growth and transformation as you transitioned into fatherhood. Through self-reflection and introspection, you explored the changes and challenges accompanying this new role, embracing the opportunity to grow and evolve as a parent and person.

Chapter 6 helped you navigate the delicate balance of work and family life, prioritizing communication and collaboration with your partner and ensuring that your family's needs were met with grace and understanding. By fostering open and honest dialogue, you strengthened your relationship and created a supportive environment where both partners could thrive.

Chapter 7 emphasized the importance of self-care and community support in maintaining one's well-being as a father. By prioritizing one's physical, emotional, and mental health, one laid the foundation for resilience and strength, ensuring

Afterword

one could show up as the best version of oneself for one's family.

And finally, in Chapter 8, you discovered the profound impact of your support on the potential postpartum depression your partner might experience. By offering love, understanding, and practical assistance, you became a pillar of strength for them, guiding them through the challenges of motherhood with compassion and grace.

Show Other Dads the Way Forward!

From the first day of fatherhood, your life is forever changed. You'll always be someone's dad now, and what an honor that is. Before you go, take a moment to share this information with more men about to set forth on this life-changing journey.

Simply by sharing your honest opinion of this book and a little about how it's helped you, you'll show other new dads where they can find all the information they need to step into fatherhood with confidence.

Thank you so much for your support. You're about to begin

Afterword

the most rewarding adventure of your life: Enjoy every moment.

To leave your review on Amazon
    https://www.amazon.com/review/create-review/?ie=UTF8&channel=glance-detail&asin=B0D7KGKP1X

Thank you for reading,
    Joshua S.

References

Adjusting to change: expecting and new dads. (n.d.). Panda. https://panda.org.au/articles/adjusting-to-change-expecting-and-new-dads/*After Baby Arrives*. (n.d.). UCLA Health. https://www.uclahealth.org/medical-services/birthplace/planning-your-childs-birth/after-baby-arrives

Allied Health. (2023, July 7). *Managing challenges faced by modern fathers*. https://pulseallied.health/challenges-faced-by-modern-fathers/

Andrews, J. D. (2023, December 28). *How to Swaddle Baby Like a Pro*. The Bump. https://www.thebump.com/a/how-to-swaddle-baby

Anzelotti, A. W. (2023, March). *Car seat safety (for parents) - KidsHealth*. https://kidshealth.org/en/parents/auto-baby-toddler.html

Asmundsson, L. (2023, June 18). *Baby milestones chart: A week-by-week guide to development*. Parents. https://www.parents.com/baby/development/growth/baby-development-week-by-week/

Balancing introducing solids with milk feeds. (2019). Pregnancybirthbaby.org. https://www.pregnancybirthbaby.org.au/balancing-introducing-solids-with-milk-feeds

Bartz, A. (2022, December 16). *The age-by-age guide to bonding with your baby*. Parents. https://www.parents.com/baby/care/american-baby-how-tos/bond-with-baby-age-guide/

Bayless, K. (2023, June 28). *Baby burping: What you should know*. Parents. https://www.parents.com/baby/care/burping/baby-burping-what-you-should-know/

Being a new parent: sex after pregnancy. (2022, December 5). NCT (National Childbirth Trust). https://www.nct.org.uk/life-parent/sex-after-baby/being-new-parent-sex-after-pregnancy

Bruce, D. F. (2022, August 23). *An overview of postpartum depression*. WebMD. https://www.webmd.com/depression/postpartum-depression

Callahan Schnabolk, L. (2023, October 30). *What happens right after baby is born?* The Bump. https://www.thebump.com/a/what-happens-after-the-baby-is-born

Carberg, J. (2023, July 23). *Statistics on postpartum depression*. PostpartumDepression.org. https://www.postpartumdepression.org/resources/statistics/

Castro, K. (2023, January 12). *Dear moms and dads, self-care is not selfish*. Wellnite. https://www.wellnite.com/post/dear-moms-and-dads-self-care-is-not-selfish

References

CDC. (2022, July 14). *How to clean, sanitize, and store infant feeding items.* https://www.cdc.gov/hygiene/childcare/clean-sanitize.html

CDC. (2019, October 1). *Signs your child is hungry or full.* https://www.cdc.gov/nutrition/infantandtoddlernutrition/mealtime/signs-your-child-is-hungry-or-full.html

Changes in your relationships after having a baby. (2019, July 16). NCT (National Childbirth Trust). https://www.nct.org.uk/life-parent/your-relationship-couple/relationship-changes/changes-your-relationships-after-having-baby

Chen, J. (2021, March 19). *Your checklist for the perfect nursery.* The Bump. https://www.thebump.com/a/creating-a-nursery

Cleaning and sterilising baby bottles. (2019). Pregnancybirthbaby.org.au. https://www.pregnancybirthbaby.org.au/cleaning-and-sterilising-baby-bottles

Communicating with your partner in the perinatal period. (n.d.). Panda. https://panda.org.au/articles/communicating-with-your-partner-in-the-perinatal-period/

Cues. (n.d.). Www.rch.org.au. https://www.rch.org.au/cocoon/project/getting-to-know-baby/Cues/

Curran, E. J. (2023, April 4). *How to massage a baby.* Parents. https://www.parents.com/baby/care/newborn/how-to-massage-baby/

Davies, A. (2019, February 21). *Rooming in with baby vs hospital nursery: The pros and cons.* Www.thebump.com. https://www.thebump.com/a/rooming-in-vs-nursery-care

Dressing a newborn — tips and safety advice. (2023, February 9). Pregnancy Birth & Baby.org.au. https://www.pregnancybirthbaby.org.au/dressing-a-newborn

Dumaplin, C. (2023, November 30). *How to play with a newborn.* Taking Cara Babies. https://takingcarababies.com/how-to-play-with-a-newborn

Geddes, J. K. (2022, August 12). *How to babyproof every room of the house.* What to Expect. https://www.whattoexpect.com/nursery-decorating/childproofing-basics.aspx

Harnish, A. (2023, May 12). *How to change your baby's diaper.* What to Expect. https://www.whattoexpect.com/first-year/diapering/how-to-change-a-diaper/

Harris, N. (2022, December 5). *Baby feeding chart: How much and when to feed infants the first year.* Parents. https://www.parents.com/baby/feeding/baby-feeding-chart-how-much-and-when-to-feed-infants-the-first-year/

How to be a parenting team. (2023, November 20). NCT (National Childbirth Trust). https://www.nct.org.uk/life-parent/your-relationship-couple/relationship-changes/how-be-parenting-team

How to hold a newborn: in pictures. (n.d.). Raising Children Network. https://

References

raisingchildren.net.au/newborns/health-daily-care/holding-newborns/how-to-hold-your-newborn

How to prepare for driving home from the maternity ward. (n.d.). Be Safe. https://www.besafe.com/safety-tips/tips/going-home-from-maternity-ward/

How to start weaning - Start for life. (2023, June 13). NHS. https://www.nhs.uk/start-for-life/baby/weaning/how-to-start-weaning-your-baby/

Joormann, J. (2023, April 9). *How becoming a dad changes men.* Psychology Today. https://www.psychologytoday.com/intl/blog/thoughts-and-feelings/202304/being-more-involved-affects-new-fathers-biologically

Lawler, M. (2022, August 26). *How to start a self-care routine you'll follow.* Everyday Health. https://www.everydayhealth.com/self-care/start-a-self-care-routine/#tips-for-coping-in-uncertain-times

LoMonaco, J. L. (2022, June 17). *How your body and brain change when you become a dad.* Cradlewise.com. https://cradlewise.com/blog/how-fatherhood-changes-your-body-and-brain

Malachi, R. (2024, January 4). *8 Safest ways to hyandle a newborn baby.* MomJunction. https://www.momjunction.com/articles/ways-hold-newborn-child_0085453/

Marcin, A. (2016, August 3). *How to hold a newborn baby.* Healthline. https://www.healthline.com/health/parenting/how-to-hold-a-newborn#Step-4:-Choose-your-position

McConville, K. (2023, January 6). *How to keep the romantic spark alive after baby.* The Bump. https://www.thebump.com/a/revving-up-your-sex-life-after-baby

Miles, K. (2023, June 30). *Doctor visits for your baby's first year.* BabyCenter. https://www.babycenter.com/health/doctor-visits-and-vaccines/doctor-visits-for-your-babys-first-year_66

Morse, J. (2022, March 1). *10 tips for handling and holding a newborn.* UT Southwestern Medical Center. https://utswmed.org/medblog/newborn-holding-tips/

Murray, D. (2021, April 10). *Can all women breastfeed?* Verywell Family. https://www.verywellfamily.com/why-some-women-cant-breastfeed-4153606

NCT. (2019, August 30). *Step-by-step guide to preparing a formula feed.* https://www.nct.org.uk/baby-toddler/feeding/practical-tips/step-step-guide-preparing-formula-feed

Novak, S. (2020, December 10). *13 tips for balancing work and a new baby.* What to Expect. https://www.whattoexpect.com/first-year/baby-care/balancing-work-and-new-baby/

Postpartum depression. (2019, March). March of Dimes. https://www.marchofdimes.org/find-support/topics/postpartum/postpartum-depression

References

Proper storage and preparation of breast milk. (2022, January 24). Centers for Disease Control and Prevention. https://www.cdc.gov/breastfeeding/recommendations/handling_breastmilk.htm

Pumping and storing breastmilk. (2017, January 31). Womenshealth.gov. https://www.womenshealth.gov/breastfeeding/pumping-and-storing-breastmilk

Ruddy, E. Z. (2023, June 30). *Postpartum sex: Everything you need to know.* Parents. https://www.parents.com/parenting/relationships/sex-and-marriage-after-baby/how-to-have-great-postpartum-sex/#toc-how-will-sex-after-birth-feel

Sears, B. (2013, July 26). *Nursery care versus rooming-in.* Ask Dr Sears. https://www.askdrsears.com/topics/pregnancy-childbirth/tenth-month-postpartum/bonding-with-your-newborn/rooming-vs-nursery-care/

Segal, J., & Smith, M. (2024, February 5). *When your baby won't stop crying.* HelpGuide.org. https://www.helpguide.org/articles/parenting-family/when-your-baby-wont-stop-crying.htm

Soto, Josiah. "These Honest Fatherhood Quotes Will Resonate With Dads Everywhere." The Pioneer Woman. Last modified April 15, 2024. https://www.thepioneerwoman.com/home-lifestyle/g43850562/fatherhood-quotes/.

Shu, J. (2022, February 2). *How to pick up and put down a baby.* BabyCenter. https://www.babycenter.com/baby/newborn-baby/how-to-pick-up-and-put-down-a-baby_10379781

Sukinik, U. S. (2017, April 10). *Postpartum checklist for hospital discharge.* Birth You Desire. https://birthyoudesire.com/postpartum-checklist-for-hospital-discharge/

Taylor, M. (2022, August 8). *Night weaning — How and when to wean baby off night feedings.* Www.whattoexpect.com. https://www.whattoexpect.com/first-year/sleep/night-weaning-baby/

Tips for bottle-feeding your baby. (2020, December 6). NCT (National Childbirth Trust). https://www.nct.org.uk/baby-toddler/feeding/practical-tips/tips-for-bottle-feeding-your-baby

Tips for brushing baby & toddler teeth. (2020, September 10). Hurst Pediatric Dentistry. https://hurstpediatricdentistry.com/2020/09/10/tips-for-brushing-baby-toddler-teeth/

Top challenges every dad face - Difficulties of being a father. (2023, May 23). Www.daduniversity.com. https://www.daduniversity.com/blog/top-challenges-every-dad-face

Weaning. (2022, November). Pregnancy Birth Baby. https://www.pregnancybirthbaby.org.au/weaning

Weishaupt, J. (2024, February 16). *What to put in a baby first aid kit.* WebMD. https://www.webmd.com/parenting/baby/what-to-put-in-baby-first-aid-kit

References

Why dads need support, too! (2023, May 9). The Mindful Birth Group. https://www.themindfulbirthgroup.com/parents/blog/top-five-reasons-why-all-dads-need-support-too/

Wisner, W. (2023, December 6). *9 Essential products and accessories you need for breastfeeding*. Parents. https://www.parents.com/what-do-i-need-to-buy-for-breastfeeding-8407663

Yang, S. (2017, March 2). *Baby's checkup schedule*. The Bump. https://www.thebump.com/a/new-baby-doctor-visit-checklist

Young-Hoon, K.-N., & Mackie, C. (2012). *The importance of child car seats and current challenges with their use*. Paediatrics & Child Health, *17*(9), 483–484. https://doi.org/10.1093/pch/17.9.483

About the Author

Joshua has been a registered nurse since 2010. He discovered a passion for writing in grade school, finding joy in expressing himself through words, which is felt in his writing.

Joshua's love for helping others extends beyond his nursing career and personal life. An avid traveler, he enjoys exploring the world, seeking adventures, and venturing off the beaten path. After all, You can't have a favorite place until you have seen them all.

Joshua Lewis Sink, BSN, RN, is an emerging author of spy help guides. This is Joshua's first book.

Through his roles as a nurse, writer, and adventurer, Joshua continually seeks ways to positively impact those around him and embrace life's diverse experiences.

Also by Joshua Lewis Sink, BSN, RN

Instruction Manual for First-Time Moms

Foster Bonding with your Newborn, from Sleepless Nights to Peaceful Mornings and Maintain your Identity - Even if You Never Held a Baby Before

Scan here to Buy on Amazon :)

Printed in Great Britain
by Amazon